C-1563   CAREER EXAMINATION SERIES

*This is your*
*PASSBOOK for...*

# Park Supervisor/I

*Test Preparation Study Guide*
*Questions & Answers*

NATIONAL LEARNING CORPORATION®

# COPYRIGHT NOTICE

This book is SOLELY intended for, is sold ONLY to, and its use is RESTRICTED to individual, bona fide applicants or candidates who qualify by virtue of having seriously filed applications for appropriate license, certificate, professional and/or promotional advancement, higher school matriculation, scholarship, or other legitimate requirements of education and/or governmental authorities.

This book is NOT intended for use, class instruction, tutoring, training, duplication, copying, reprinting, excerption, or adaptation, etc., by:

1) Other publishers
2) Proprietors and/or Instructors of "Coaching" and/or Preparatory Courses
3) Personnel and/or Training Divisions of commercial, industrial, and governmental organizations
4) Schools, colleges, or universities and/or their departments and staffs, including teachers and other personnel
5) Testing Agencies or Bureaus
6) Study groups which seek by the purchase of a single volume to copy and/or duplicate and/or adapt this material for use by the group as a whole without having purchased individual volumes for each of the members of the group
7) Et al.

Such persons would be in violation of appropriate Federal and State statutes.

PROVISION OF LICENSING AGREEMENTS – Recognized educational, commercial, industrial, and governmental institutions and organizations, and others legitimately engaged in educational pursuits, including training, testing, and measurement activities, may address request for a licensing agreement to the copyright owners, who will determine whether, and under what conditions, including fees and charges, the materials in this book may be used them. In other words, a licensing facility exists for the legitimate use of the material in this book on other than an individual basis. However, it is asseverated and affirmed here that the material in this book CANNOT be used without the receipt of the express permission of such a licensing agreement from the Publishers. Inquiries re licensing should be addressed to the company, attention rights and permissions department.

All rights reserved, including the right of reproduction in whole or in part, in any form or by any means, electronic or mechanical, including photocopying, recording, or by any information storage and retrieval system, without permission in writing from the Publisher.

Copyright © 2024 by
## National Learning Corporation

212 Michael Drive, Syosset, NY 11791
(516) 921-8888 • www.passbooks.com
E-mail: info@passbooks.com

PUBLISHED IN THE UNITED STATES OF AMERICA

# PASSBOOK® SERIES

THE *PASSBOOK® SERIES* has been created to prepare applicants and candidates for the ultimate academic battlefield – the examination room.

At some time in our lives, each and every one of us may be required to take an examination – for validation, matriculation, admission, qualification, registration, certification, or licensure.

Based on the assumption that every applicant or candidate has met the basic formal educational standards, has taken the required number of courses, and read the necessary texts, the *PASSBOOK® SERIES* furnishes the one special preparation which may assure passing with confidence, instead of failing with insecurity. Examination questions – together with answers – are furnished as the basic vehicle for study so that the mysteries of the examination and its compounding difficulties may be eliminated or diminished by a sure method.

This book is meant to help you pass your examination provided that you qualify and are serious in your objective.

The entire field is reviewed through the huge store of content information which is succinctly presented through a provocative and challenging approach – the question-and-answer method.

A climate of success is established by furnishing the correct answers at the end of each test.

You soon learn to recognize types of questions, forms of questions, and patterns of questioning. You may even begin to anticipate expected outcomes.

You perceive that many questions are repeated or adapted so that you can gain acute insights, which may enable you to score many sure points.

You learn how to confront new questions, or types of questions, and to attack them confidently and work out the correct answers.

You note objectives and emphases, and recognize pitfalls and dangers, so that you may make positive educational adjustments.

Moreover, you are kept fully informed in relation to new concepts, methods, practices, and directions in the field.

You discover that you are actually taking the examination all the time: you are preparing for the examination by "taking" an examination, not by reading extraneous and/or supererogatory textbooks.

In short, this PASSBOOK®, used directedly, should be an important factor in helping you to pass your test.

# PARK SUPERVISOR

DUTIES:
Supervises the operation and maintenance of a moderate to small-sized park. Performs related duties as required.

SCOPE OF THE EXAMINATION:
The written test will be designed to test for knowledge, skills, and/or abilities in such areas as:
1. **Educating and Interacting with the Public** — These questions test Few knowledge of techniques used to interact effectively with individuals and/or community groups, to educate or inform them about topics of concern, to publicize or clarify agency programs or policies, to negotiate conflicts or resolve complaints, and to represent one's agency or program in a manner in keeping with good public relations practices, Questions may also cover interacting with others in cooperative efforts of public outreach or service,
2. **Maintenance of Buildings and Equipment** — These questions test for knowledge of the principles and practices involved in the overall maintenance, construction, and upkeep of the typical structures, buildings, and equipment found in park facilities; and may include such areas as proper maintenance and repair of buildings, roadways, trails, flood control and drainage structures, minor mechanical and electrical systems maintenance. and safe operating practices.
3. **Operation of Park Facilities** — These questions test for knowledge of the practices and procedures involved in operating park facilities and may include such typical areas as job safety, grounds and equipment maintenance, prioritizing work schedules, inspection and repair of park playgrounds, picnic areas, swimming facilities, public restrooms, hiking trails, and other park facilities. water and wastewater line repair, proper use of hand and power tools, revenue collection, customer and employee relations, and proper handling of emergency situations.
4. **Installation, Maintenance, and Repair of Recreation Areas** — These questions test for knowledge of the principles and practices involved in the installation, upkeep, maintenance and repair of park and recreation facilities, including such areas as picnic facilities, playgrounds, athletic and playing fields. trails and walkways, sanitary facilities, and lawn care and grounds maintenance.
5. **Supervision** — These questions test for knowledge of the principles and practices employed in planning, organizing, and controlling the activities of a work unit toward predetermined objectives. The concepts covered, usually in a situational question format, include such topics as assigning and reviewing work; evaluating performance; maintaining work standards; motivating and developing subordinates; implementing procedural change; increasing efficiency: and dealing with problems of absenteeism, morale, and discipline.
6. **Understanding and Interpreting Written Material** — These questions test how well you comprehend written material. You will be provided with brief reading selections and will be asked questions about the selections. All the information required to answer the questions will he presented in the selections; you will not be required to have any special knowledge relating to the subject areas of the selections,

# HOW TO TAKE A TEST

I. YOU MUST PASS AN EXAMINATION

## A. WHAT EVERY CANDIDATE SHOULD KNOW

Examination applicants often ask us for help in preparing for the written test. What can I study in advance? What kinds of questions will be asked? How will the test be given? How will the papers be graded?

As an applicant for a civil service examination, you may be wondering about some of these things. Our purpose here is to suggest effective methods of advance study and to describe civil service examinations.

Your chances for success on this examination can be increased if you know how to prepare. Those "pre-examination jitters" can be reduced if you know what to expect. You can even experience an adventure in good citizenship if you know why civil service exams are given.

## B. WHY ARE CIVIL SERVICE EXAMINATIONS GIVEN?

Civil service examinations are important to you in two ways. As a citizen, you want public jobs filled by employees who know how to do their work. As a job seeker, you want a fair chance to compete for that job on an equal footing with other candidates. The best-known means of accomplishing this two-fold goal is the competitive examination.

Exams are widely publicized throughout the nation. They may be administered for jobs in federal, state, city, municipal, town or village governments or agencies.

Any citizen may apply, with some limitations, such as the age or residence of applicants. Your experience and education may be reviewed to see whether you meet the requirements for the particular examination. When these requirements exist, they are reasonable and applied consistently to all applicants. Thus, a competitive examination may cause you some uneasiness now, but it is your privilege and safeguard.

## C. HOW ARE CIVIL SERVICE EXAMS DEVELOPED?

Examinations are carefully written by trained technicians who are specialists in the field known as "psychological measurement," in consultation with recognized authorities in the field of work that the test will cover. These experts recommend the subject matter areas or skills to be tested; only those knowledges or skills important to your success on the job are included. The most reliable books and source materials available are used as references. Together, the experts and technicians judge the difficulty level of the questions.

Test technicians know how to phrase questions so that the problem is clearly stated. Their ethics do not permit "trick" or "catch" questions. Questions may have been tried out on sample groups, or subjected to statistical analysis, to determine their usefulness.

Written tests are often used in combination with performance tests, ratings of training and experience, and oral interviews. All of these measures combine to form the best-known means of finding the right person for the right job.

## II. HOW TO PASS THE WRITTEN TEST

### A. NATURE OF THE EXAMINATION

To prepare intelligently for civil service examinations, you should know how they differ from school examinations you have taken. In school you were assigned certain definite pages to read or subjects to cover. The examination questions were quite detailed and usually emphasized memory. Civil service exams, on the other hand, try to discover your present ability to perform the duties of a position, plus your potentiality to learn these duties. In other words, a civil service exam attempts to predict how successful you will be. Questions cover such a broad area that they cannot be as minute and detailed as school exam questions.

In the public service similar kinds of work, or positions, are grouped together in one "class." This process is known as *position-classification*. All the positions in a class are paid according to the salary range for that class. One class title covers all of these positions, and they are all tested by the same examination.

### B. FOUR BASIC STEPS

#### 1) Study the announcement

How, then, can you know what subjects to study? Our best answer is: "Learn as much as possible about the class of positions for which you've applied." The exam will test the knowledge, skills and abilities needed to do the work.

Your most valuable source of information about the position you want is the official exam announcement. This announcement lists the training and experience qualifications. Check these standards and apply only if you come reasonably close to meeting them.

The brief description of the position in the examination announcement offers some clues to the subjects which will be tested. Think about the job itself. Review the duties in your mind. Can you perform them, or are there some in which you are rusty? Fill in the blank spots in your preparation.

Many jurisdictions preview the written test in the exam announcement by including a section called "Knowledge and Abilities Required," "Scope of the Examination," or some similar heading. Here you will find out specifically what fields will be tested.

#### 2) Review your own background

Once you learn in general what the position is all about, and what you need to know to do the work, ask yourself which subjects you already know fairly well and which need improvement. You may wonder whether to concentrate on improving your strong areas or on building some background in your fields of weakness. When the announcement has specified "some knowledge" or "considerable knowledge," or has used adjectives like "beginning principles of..." or "advanced ... methods," you can get a clue as to the number and difficulty of questions to be asked in any given field. More questions, and hence broader coverage, would be included for those subjects which are more important in the work. Now weigh your strengths and weaknesses against the job requirements and prepare accordingly.

#### 3) Determine the level of the position

Another way to tell how intensively you should prepare is to understand the level of the job for which you are applying. Is it the entering level? In other words, is this the position in which beginners in a field of work are hired? Or is it an intermediate or advanced level? Sometimes this is indicated by such words as "Junior" or "Senior" in the class title. Other jurisdictions use Roman numerals to designate the level – Clerk I, Clerk II, for example. The word "Supervisor" sometimes appears in the title. If the level is not indicated by the title, check the description of duties. Will you be working under very close supervision, or will you have responsibility for independent decisions in this work?

### 4) Choose appropriate study materials

Now that you know the subjects to be examined and the relative amount of each subject to be covered, you can choose suitable study materials. For beginning level jobs, or even advanced ones, if you have a pronounced weakness in some aspect of your training, read a modern, standard textbook in that field. Be sure it is up to date and has general coverage. Such books are normally available at your library, and the librarian will be glad to help you locate one. For entry-level positions, questions of appropriate difficulty are chosen – neither highly advanced questions, nor those too simple. Such questions require careful thought but not advanced training.

If the position for which you are applying is technical or advanced, you will read more advanced, specialized material. If you are already familiar with the basic principles of your field, elementary textbooks would waste your time. Concentrate on advanced textbooks and technical periodicals. Think through the concepts and review difficult problems in your field.

These are all general sources. You can get more ideas on your own initiative, following these leads. For example, training manuals and publications of the government agency which employs workers in your field can be useful, particularly for technical and professional positions. A letter or visit to the government department involved may result in more specific study suggestions, and certainly will provide you with a more definite idea of the exact nature of the position you are seeking.

## III. KINDS OF TESTS

Tests are used for purposes other than measuring knowledge and ability to perform specified duties. For some positions, it is equally important to test ability to make adjustments to new situations or to profit from training. In others, basic mental abilities not dependent on information are essential. Questions which test these things may not appear as pertinent to the duties of the position as those which test for knowledge and information. Yet they are often highly important parts of a fair examination. For very general questions, it is almost impossible to help you direct your study efforts. What we can do is to point out some of the more common of these general abilities needed in public service positions and describe some typical questions.

1) General information

Broad, general information has been found useful for predicting job success in some kinds of work. This is tested in a variety of ways, from vocabulary lists to questions about current events. Basic background in some field of work, such as sociology or economics, may be sampled in a group of questions. Often these are principles which have become familiar to most persons through exposure rather than through formal training. It is difficult to advise you how to study for these questions; being alert to the world around you is our best suggestion.

2) Verbal ability

An example of an ability needed in many positions is verbal or language ability. Verbal ability is, in brief, the ability to use and understand words. Vocabulary and grammar tests are typical measures of this ability. Reading comprehension or paragraph interpretation questions are common in many kinds of civil service tests. You are given a paragraph of written material and asked to find its central meaning.

3) Numerical ability

Number skills can be tested by the familiar arithmetic problem, by checking paired lists of numbers to see which are alike and which are different, or by interpreting charts and graphs. In the latter test, a graph may be printed in the test booklet which you are asked to use as the basis for answering questions.

4) Observation

A popular test for law-enforcement positions is the observation test. A picture is shown to you for several minutes, then taken away. Questions about the picture test your ability to observe both details and larger elements.

5) Following directions

In many positions in the public service, the employee must be able to carry out written instructions dependably and accurately. You may be given a chart with several columns, each column listing a variety of information. The questions require you to carry out directions involving the information given in the chart.

6) Skills and aptitudes

Performance tests effectively measure some manual skills and aptitudes. When the skill is one in which you are trained, such as typing or shorthand, you can practice. These tests are often very much like those given in business school or high school courses. For many of the other skills and aptitudes, however, no short-time preparation can be made. Skills and abilities natural to you or that you have developed throughout your lifetime are being tested.

Many of the general questions just described provide all the data needed to answer the questions and ask you to use your reasoning ability to find the answers. Your best preparation for these tests, as well as for tests of facts and ideas, is to be at your physical and mental best. You, no doubt, have your own methods of getting into an exam-taking mood and keeping "in shape." The next section lists some ideas on this subject.

IV. KINDS OF QUESTIONS

Only rarely is the "essay" question, which you answer in narrative form, used in civil service tests. Civil service tests are usually of the short-answer type. Full instructions for answering these questions will be given to you at the examination. But in case this is your first experience with short-answer questions and separate answer sheets, here is what you need to know:

1) **Multiple-choice Questions**

Most popular of the short-answer questions is the "multiple choice" or "best answer" question. It can be used, for example, to test for factual knowledge, ability to solve problems or judgment in meeting situations found at work.

A multiple-choice question is normally one of three types—
- It can begin with an incomplete statement followed by several possible endings. You are to find the one ending which *best* completes the statement, although some of the others may not be entirely wrong.
- It can also be a complete statement in the form of a question which is answered by choosing one of the statements listed.

- It can be in the form of a problem – again you select the best answer.

Here is an example of a multiple-choice question with a discussion which should give you some clues as to the method for choosing the right answer:

When an employee has a complaint about his assignment, the action which will *best* help him overcome his difficulty is to
- A. discuss his difficulty with his coworkers
- B. take the problem to the head of the organization
- C. take the problem to the person who gave him the assignment
- D. say nothing to anyone about his complaint

In answering this question, you should study each of the choices to find which is best. Consider choice "A" – Certainly an employee may discuss his complaint with fellow employees, but no change or improvement can result, and the complaint remains unresolved. Choice "B" is a poor choice since the head of the organization probably does not know what assignment you have been given, and taking your problem to him is known as "going over the head" of the supervisor. The supervisor, or person who made the assignment, is the person who can clarify it or correct any injustice. Choice "C" is, therefore, correct. To say nothing, as in choice "D," is unwise. Supervisors have and interest in knowing the problems employees are facing, and the employee is seeking a solution to his problem.

## 2) True/False Questions

The "true/false" or "right/wrong" form of question is sometimes used. Here a complete statement is given. Your job is to decide whether the statement is right or wrong.

SAMPLE: A roaming cell-phone call to a nearby city costs less than a non-roaming call to a distant city.

This statement is wrong, or false, since roaming calls are more expensive.

This is not a complete list of all possible question forms, although most of the others are variations of these common types. You will always get complete directions for answering questions. Be sure you understand *how* to mark your answers – ask questions until you do.

## V. RECORDING YOUR ANSWERS

Computer terminals are used more and more today for many different kinds of exams.
For an examination with very few applicants, you may be told to record your answers in the test booklet itself. Separate answer sheets are much more common. If this separate answer sheet is to be scored by machine – and this is often the case – it is highly important that you mark your answers correctly in order to get credit.

An electronic scoring machine is often used in civil service offices because of the speed with which papers can be scored. Machine-scored answer sheets must be marked with a pencil, which will be given to you. This pencil has a high graphite content which responds to the electronic scoring machine. As a matter of fact, stray dots may register as answers, so do not let your pencil rest on the answer sheet while you are pondering the correct answer. Also, if your pencil lead breaks or is otherwise defective, ask for another.

Since the answer sheet will be dropped in a slot in the scoring machine, be careful not to bend the corners or get the paper crumpled.

The answer sheet normally has five vertical columns of numbers, with 30 numbers to a column. These numbers correspond to the question numbers in your test booklet. After each number, going across the page are four or five pairs of dotted lines. These short dotted lines have small letters or numbers above them. The first two pairs may also have a "T" or "F" above the letters. This indicates that the first two pairs only are to be used if the questions are of the true-false type. If the questions are multiple choice, disregard the "T" and "F" and pay attention only to the small letters or numbers.

Answer your questions in the manner of the sample that follows:

32. The largest city in the United States is
    A. Washington, D.C.
    B. New York City
    C. Chicago
    D. Detroit
    E. San Francisco

1) Choose the answer you think is best. (New York City is the largest, so "B" is correct.)
2) Find the row of dotted lines numbered the same as the question you are answering. (Find row number 32)
3) Find the pair of dotted lines corresponding to the answer. (Find the pair of lines under the mark "B.")
4) Make a solid black mark between the dotted lines.


## VI. BEFORE THE TEST

Common sense will help you find procedures to follow to get ready for an examination. Too many of us, however, overlook these sensible measures. Indeed, nervousness and fatigue have been found to be the most serious reasons why applicants fail to do their best on civil service tests. Here is a list of reminders:

- Begin your preparation early – Don't wait until the last minute to go scurrying around for books and materials or to find out what the position is all about.
- Prepare continuously – An hour a night for a week is better than an all-night cram session. This has been definitely established. What is more, a night a week for a month will return better dividends than crowding your study into a shorter period of time.
- Locate the place of the exam – You have been sent a notice telling you when and where to report for the examination. If the location is in a different town or otherwise unfamiliar to you, it would be well to inquire the best route and learn something about the building.
- Relax the night before the test – Allow your mind to rest. Do not study at all that night. Plan some mild recreation or diversion; then go to bed early and get a good night's sleep.
- Get up early enough to make a leisurely trip to the place for the test – This way unforeseen events, traffic snarls, unfamiliar buildings, etc. will not upset you.
- Dress comfortably – A written test is not a fashion show. You will be known by number and not by name, so wear something comfortable.

- Leave excess paraphernalia at home – Shopping bags and odd bundles will get in your way. You need bring only the items mentioned in the official notice you received; usually everything you need is provided. Do not bring reference books to the exam. They will only confuse those last minutes and be taken away from you when in the test room.
- Arrive somewhat ahead of time – If because of transportation schedules you must get there very early, bring a newspaper or magazine to take your mind off yourself while waiting.
- Locate the examination room – When you have found the proper room, you will be directed to the seat or part of the room where you will sit. Sometimes you are given a sheet of instructions to read while you are waiting. Do not fill out any forms until you are told to do so; just read them and be prepared.
- Relax and prepare to listen to the instructions
- If you have any physical problem that may keep you from doing your best, be sure to tell the test administrator. If you are sick or in poor health, you really cannot do your best on the exam. You can come back and take the test some other time.

## VII. AT THE TEST

The day of the test is here and you have the test booklet in your hand. The temptation to get going is very strong. Caution! There is more to success than knowing the right answers. You must know how to identify your papers and understand variations in the type of short-answer question used in this particular examination. Follow these suggestions for maximum results from your efforts:

### 1) Cooperate with the monitor

The test administrator has a duty to create a situation in which you can be as much at ease as possible. He will give instructions, tell you when to begin, check to see that you are marking your answer sheet correctly, and so on. He is not there to guard you, although he will see that your competitors do not take unfair advantage. He wants to help you do your best.

### 2) Listen to all instructions

Don't jump the gun! Wait until you understand all directions. In most civil service tests you get more time than you need to answer the questions. So don't be in a hurry. Read each word of instructions until you clearly understand the meaning. Study the examples, listen to all announcements and follow directions. Ask questions if you do not understand what to do.

### 3) Identify your papers

Civil service exams are usually identified by number only. You will be assigned a number; you must not put your name on your test papers. Be sure to copy your number correctly. Since more than one exam may be given, copy your exact examination title.

### 4) Plan your time

Unless you are told that a test is a "speed" or "rate of work" test, speed itself is usually not important. Time enough to answer all the questions will be provided, but this does not mean that you have all day. An overall time limit has been set. Divide the total time (in minutes) by the number of questions to determine the approximate time you have for each question.

### 5) Do not linger over difficult questions

If you come across a difficult question, mark it with a paper clip (useful to have along) and come back to it when you have been through the booklet. One caution if you do this – be sure to skip a number on your answer sheet as well. Check often to be sure that you have not lost your place and that you are marking in the row numbered the same as the question you are answering.

### 6) Read the questions

Be sure you know what the question asks! Many capable people are unsuccessful because they failed to *read* the questions correctly.

### 7) Answer all questions

Unless you have been instructed that a penalty will be deducted for incorrect answers, it is better to guess than to omit a question.

### 8) Speed tests

It is often better NOT to guess on speed tests. It has been found that on timed tests people are tempted to spend the last few seconds before time is called in marking answers at random – without even reading them – in the hope of picking up a few extra points. To discourage this practice, the instructions may warn you that your score will be "corrected" for guessing. That is, a penalty will be applied. The incorrect answers will be deducted from the correct ones, or some other penalty formula will be used.

### 9) Review your answers

If you finish before time is called, go back to the questions you guessed or omitted to give them further thought. Review other answers if you have time.

### 10) Return your test materials

If you are ready to leave before others have finished or time is called, take ALL your materials to the monitor and leave quietly. Never take any test material with you. The monitor can discover whose papers are not complete, and taking a test booklet may be grounds for disqualification.

## VIII. EXAMINATION TECHNIQUES

1) Read the general instructions carefully. These are usually printed on the first page of the exam booklet. As a rule, these instructions refer to the timing of the examination; the fact that you should not start work until the signal and must stop work at a signal, etc. If there are any *special* instructions, such as a choice of questions to be answered, make sure that you note this instruction carefully.

2) When you are ready to start work on the examination, that is as soon as the signal has been given, read the instructions to each question booklet, underline any key words or phrases, such as *least, best, outline, describe* and the like. In this way you will tend to answer as requested rather than discover on reviewing your paper that you *listed without describing*, that you selected the *worst* choice rather than the *best* choice, etc.

3) If the examination is of the objective or multiple-choice type – that is, each question will also give a series of possible answers: A, B, C or D, and you are called upon to select the best answer and write the letter next to that answer on your answer paper – it is advisable to start answering each question in turn. There may be anywhere from 50 to 100 such questions in the three or four hours allotted and you can see how much time would be taken if you read through all the questions before beginning to answer any. Furthermore, if you come across a question or group of questions which you know would be difficult to answer, it would undoubtedly affect your handling of all the other questions.

4) If the examination is of the essay type and contains but a few questions, it is a moot point as to whether you should read all the questions before starting to answer any one. Of course, if you are given a choice – say five out of seven and the like – then it is essential to read all the questions so you can eliminate the two that are most difficult. If, however, you are asked to answer all the questions, there may be danger in trying to answer the easiest one first because you may find that you will spend too much time on it. The best technique is to answer the first question, then proceed to the second, etc.

5) Time your answers. Before the exam begins, write down the time it started, then add the time allowed for the examination and write down the time it must be completed, then divide the time available somewhat as follows:
    - If 3-1/2 hours are allowed, that would be 210 minutes. If you have 80 objective-type questions, that would be an average of 2-1/2 minutes per question. Allow yourself no more than 2 minutes per question, or a total of 160 minutes, which will permit about 50 minutes to review.
    - If for the time allotment of 210 minutes there are 7 essay questions to answer, that would average about 30 minutes a question. Give yourself only 25 minutes per question so that you have about 35 minutes to review.

6) The most important instruction is to *read each question* and make sure you know what is wanted. The second most important instruction is to *time yourself properly* so that you answer every question. The third most important instruction is to *answer every question*. Guess if you have to but include something for each question. Remember that you will receive no credit for a blank and will probably receive some credit if you write something in answer to an essay question. If you guess a letter – say "B" for a multiple-choice question – you may have guessed right. If you leave a blank as an answer to a multiple-choice question, the examiners may respect your feelings but it will not add a point to your score. Some exams may penalize you for wrong answers, so in such cases *only*, you may not want to guess unless you have some basis for your answer.

7) Suggestions
    a. Objective-type questions
        1. Examine the question booklet for proper sequence of pages and questions
        2. Read all instructions carefully
        3. Skip any question which seems too difficult; return to it after all other questions have been answered
        4. Apportion your time properly; do not spend too much time on any single question or group of questions

5. Note and underline key words – *all, most, fewest, least, best, worst, same, opposite,* etc.
6. Pay particular attention to negatives
7. Note unusual option, e.g., unduly long, short, complex, different or similar in content to the body of the question
8. Observe the use of "hedging" words – *probably, may, most likely,* etc.
9. Make sure that your answer is put next to the same number as the question
10. Do not second-guess unless you have good reason to believe the second answer is definitely more correct
11. Cross out original answer if you decide another answer is more accurate; do not erase until you are ready to hand your paper in
12. Answer all questions; guess unless instructed otherwise
13. Leave time for review

  b. Essay questions
    1. Read each question carefully
    2. Determine exactly what is wanted. Underline key words or phrases.
    3. Decide on outline or paragraph answer
    4. Include many different points and elements unless asked to develop any one or two points or elements
    5. Show impartiality by giving pros and cons unless directed to select one side only
    6. Make and write down any assumptions you find necessary to answer the questions
    7. Watch your English, grammar, punctuation and choice of words
    8. Time your answers; don't crowd material

8) Answering the essay question

Most essay questions can be answered by framing the specific response around several key words or ideas. Here are a few such key words or ideas:

M's: manpower, materials, methods, money, management
P's: purpose, program, policy, plan, procedure, practice, problems, pitfalls, personnel, public relations

  a. Six basic steps in handling problems:
    1. Preliminary plan and background development
    2. Collect information, data and facts
    3. Analyze and interpret information, data and facts
    4. Analyze and develop solutions as well as make recommendations
    5. Prepare report and sell recommendations
    6. Install recommendations and follow up effectiveness

  b. Pitfalls to avoid
    1. *Taking things for granted* – A statement of the situation does not necessarily imply that each of the elements is necessarily true; for example, a complaint may be invalid and biased so that all that can be taken for granted is that a complaint has been registered

2. *Considering only one side of a situation* – Wherever possible, indicate several alternatives and then point out the reasons you selected the best one
3. *Failing to indicate follow up* – Whenever your answer indicates action on your part, make certain that you will take proper follow-up action to see how successful your recommendations, procedures or actions turn out to be
4. *Taking too long in answering any single question* – Remember to time your answers properly

## IX. AFTER THE TEST

Scoring procedures differ in detail among civil service jurisdictions although the general principles are the same. Whether the papers are hand-scored or graded by machine we have described, they are nearly always graded by number. That is, the person who marks the paper knows only the number – never the name – of the applicant. Not until all the papers have been graded will they be matched with names. If other tests, such as training and experience or oral interview ratings have been given, scores will be combined. Different parts of the examination usually have different weights. For example, the written test might count 60 percent of the final grade, and a rating of training and experience 40 percent. In many jurisdictions, veterans will have a certain number of points added to their grades.

After the final grade has been determined, the names are placed in grade order and an eligible list is established. There are various methods for resolving ties between those who get the same final grade – probably the most common is to place first the name of the person whose application was received first. Job offers are made from the eligible list in the order the names appear on it. You will be notified of your grade and your rank as soon as all these computations have been made. This will be done as rapidly as possible.

People who are found to meet the requirements in the announcement are called "eligibles." Their names are put on a list of eligible candidates. An eligible's chances of getting a job depend on how high he stands on this list and how fast agencies are filling jobs from the list.

When a job is to be filled from a list of eligibles, the agency asks for the names of people on the list of eligibles for that job. When the civil service commission receives this request, it sends to the agency the names of the three people highest on this list. Or, if the job to be filled has specialized requirements, the office sends the agency the names of the top three persons who meet these requirements from the general list.

The appointing officer makes a choice from among the three people whose names were sent to him. If the selected person accepts the appointment, the names of the others are put back on the list to be considered for future openings.

That is the rule in hiring from all kinds of eligible lists, whether they are for typist, carpenter, chemist, or something else. For every vacancy, the appointing officer has his choice of any one of the top three eligibles on the list. This explains why the person whose name is on top of the list sometimes does not get an appointment when some of the persons lower on the list do. If the appointing officer chooses the second or third eligible, the No. 1 eligible does not get a job at once, but stays on the list until he is appointed or the list is terminated.

# X. HOW TO PASS THE INTERVIEW TEST

The examination for which you applied requires an oral interview test. You have already taken the written test and you are now being called for the interview test – the final part of the formal examination.

You may think that it is not possible to prepare for an interview test and that there are no procedures to follow during an interview. Our purpose is to point out some things you can do in advance that will help you and some good rules to follow and pitfalls to avoid while you are being interviewed.

*What is an interview supposed to test?*

The written examination is designed to test the technical knowledge and competence of the candidate; the oral is designed to evaluate intangible qualities, not readily measured otherwise, and to establish a list showing the relative fitness of each candidate – as measured against his competitors – for the position sought. Scoring is not on the basis of "right" and "wrong," but on a sliding scale of values ranging from "not passable" to "outstanding." As a matter of fact, it is possible to achieve a relatively low score without a single "incorrect" answer because of evident weakness in the qualities being measured.

Occasionally, an examination may consist entirely of an oral test – either an individual or a group oral. In such cases, information is sought concerning the technical knowledges and abilities of the candidate, since there has been no written examination for this purpose. More commonly, however, an oral test is used to supplement a written examination.

*Who conducts interviews?*

The composition of oral boards varies among different jurisdictions. In nearly all, a representative of the personnel department serves as chairman. One of the members of the board may be a representative of the department in which the candidate would work. In some cases, "outside experts" are used, and, frequently, a businessman or some other representative of the general public is asked to serve. Labor and management or other special groups may be represented. The aim is to secure the services of experts in the appropriate field.

However the board is composed, it is a good idea (and not at all improper or unethical) to ascertain in advance of the interview who the members are and what groups they represent. When you are introduced to them, you will have some idea of their backgrounds and interests, and at least you will not stutter and stammer over their names.

*What should be done before the interview?*

While knowledge about the board members is useful and takes some of the surprise element out of the interview, there is other preparation which is more substantive. It *is* possible to prepare for an oral interview – in several ways:

**1) Keep a copy of your application and review it carefully before the interview**

This may be the only document before the oral board, and the starting point of the interview. Know what education and experience you have listed there, and the sequence and dates of all of it. Sometimes the board will ask you to review the highlights of your experience for them; you should not have to hem and haw doing it.

**2) Study the class specification and the examination announcement**

Usually, the oral board has one or both of these to guide them. The qualities, characteristics or knowledges required by the position sought are stated in these documents. They offer valuable clues as to the nature of the oral interview. For example, if the job involves supervisory responsibilities, the announcement will usually indicate that knowledge of modern supervisory methods and the qualifications of the candidate as a supervisor will be tested. If so, you can expect such questions, frequently in the form of a hypothetical situation which you are expected to solve. NEVER go into an oral without knowledge of the duties and responsibilities of the job you seek.

### 3) Think through each qualification required

Try to visualize the kind of questions you would ask if you were a board member. How well could you answer them? Try especially to appraise your own knowledge and background in each area, *measured against the job sought*, and identify any areas in which you are weak. Be critical and realistic – do not flatter yourself.

### 4) Do some general reading in areas in which you feel you may be weak

For example, if the job involves supervision and your past experience has NOT, some general reading in supervisory methods and practices, particularly in the field of human relations, might be useful. Do NOT study agency procedures or detailed manuals. The oral board will be testing your understanding and capacity, not your memory.

### 5) Get a good night's sleep and watch your general health and mental attitude

You will want a clear head at the interview. Take care of a cold or any other minor ailment, and of course, no hangovers.

*What should be done on the day of the interview?*

Now comes the day of the interview itself. Give yourself plenty of time to get there. Plan to arrive somewhat ahead of the scheduled time, particularly if your appointment is in the fore part of the day. If a previous candidate fails to appear, the board might be ready for you a bit early. By early afternoon an oral board is almost invariably behind schedule if there are many candidates, and you may have to wait. Take along a book or magazine to read, or your application to review, but leave any extraneous material in the waiting room when you go in for your interview. In any event, relax and compose yourself.

The matter of dress is important. The board is forming impressions about you – from your experience, your manners, your attitude, and your appearance. Give your personal appearance careful attention. Dress your best, but not your flashiest. Choose conservative, appropriate clothing, and be sure it is immaculate. This is a business interview, and your appearance should indicate that you regard it as such. Besides, being well groomed and properly dressed will help boost your confidence.

Sooner or later, someone will call your name and escort you into the interview room. *This is it.* From here on you are on your own. It is too late for any more preparation. But remember, you asked for this opportunity to prove your fitness, and you are here because your request was granted.

*What happens when you go in?*

The usual sequence of events will be as follows: The clerk (who is often the board stenographer) will introduce you to the chairman of the oral board, who will introduce you to the other members of the board. Acknowledge the introductions before you sit down. Do not be surprised if you find a microphone facing you or a stenotypist sitting by. Oral interviews are usually recorded in the event of an appeal or other review.

Usually the chairman of the board will open the interview by reviewing the highlights of your education and work experience from your application – primarily for the benefit of the other members of the board, as well as to get the material into the record. Do not interrupt or comment unless there is an error or significant misinterpretation; if that is the case, do not hesitate. But do not quibble about insignificant matters. Also, he will usually ask you some question about your education, experience or your present job – partly to get you to start talking and to establish the interviewing "rapport." He may start the actual questioning, or turn it over to one of the other members. Frequently, each member undertakes the questioning on a particular area, one in which he is perhaps most competent, so you can expect each member to participate in the examination. Because time is limited, you may also expect some rather abrupt switches in the direction the questioning takes, so do not be upset by it. Normally, a board member will not pursue a single line of questioning unless he discovers a particular strength or weakness.

After each member has participated, the chairman will usually ask whether any member has any further questions, then will ask you if you have anything you wish to add. Unless you are expecting this question, it may floor you. Worse, it may start you off on an extended, extemporaneous speech. The board is not usually seeking more information. The question is principally to offer you a last opportunity to present further qualifications or to indicate that you have nothing to add. So, if you feel that a significant qualification or characteristic has been overlooked, it is proper to point it out in a sentence or so. Do not compliment the board on the thoroughness of their examination – they have been sketchy, and you know it. If you wish, merely say, "No thank you, I have nothing further to add." This is a point where you can "talk yourself out" of a good impression or fail to present an important bit of information. Remember, *you close the interview yourself.*

The chairman will then say, "That is all, Mr. _____, thank you." Do not be startled; the interview is over, and quicker than you think. Thank him, gather your belongings and take your leave. Save your sigh of relief for the other side of the door.


*How to put your best foot forward*

Throughout this entire process, you may feel that the board individually and collectively is trying to pierce your defenses, seek out your hidden weaknesses and embarrass and confuse you. Actually, this is not true. They are obliged to make an appraisal of your qualifications for the job you are seeking, and they want to see you in your best light. Remember, they must interview all candidates and a non-cooperative candidate may become a failure in spite of their best efforts to bring out his qualifications. Here are 15 suggestions that will help you:

**1) Be natural – Keep your attitude confident, not cocky**

If you are not confident that you can do the job, do not expect the board to be. Do not apologize for your weaknesses, try to bring out your strong points. The board is interested in a positive, not negative, presentation. Cockiness will antagonize any board member and make him wonder if you are covering up a weakness by a false show of strength.

**2) Get comfortable, but don't lounge or sprawl**

Sit erectly but not stiffly. A careless posture may lead the board to conclude that you are careless in other things, or at least that you are not impressed by the importance of the occasion. Either conclusion is natural, even if incorrect. Do not fuss with your clothing, a pencil or an ashtray. Your hands may occasionally be useful to emphasize a point; do not let them become a point of distraction.

**3) Do not wisecrack or make small talk**

This is a serious situation, and your attitude should show that you consider it as such. Further, the time of the board is limited – they do not want to waste it, and neither should you.

### 4) Do not exaggerate your experience or abilities
In the first place, from information in the application or other interviews and sources, the board may know more about you than you think. Secondly, you probably will not get away with it. An experienced board is rather adept at spotting such a situation, so do not take the chance.

### 5) If you know a board member, do not make a point of it, yet do not hide it
Certainly you are not fooling him, and probably not the other members of the board. Do not try to take advantage of your acquaintanceship – it will probably do you little good.

### 6) Do not dominate the interview
Let the board do that. They will give you the clues – do not assume that you have to do all the talking. Realize that the board has a number of questions to ask you, and do not try to take up all the interview time by showing off your extensive knowledge of the answer to the first one.

### 7) Be attentive
You only have 20 minutes or so, and you should keep your attention at its sharpest throughout. When a member is addressing a problem or question to you, give him your undivided attention. Address your reply principally to him, but do not exclude the other board members.

### 8) Do not interrupt
A board member may be stating a problem for you to analyze. He will ask you a question when the time comes. Let him state the problem, and wait for the question.

### 9) Make sure you understand the question
Do not try to answer until you are sure what the question is. If it is not clear, restate it in your own words or ask the board member to clarify it for you. However, do not haggle about minor elements.

### 10) Reply promptly but not hastily
A common entry on oral board rating sheets is "candidate responded readily," or "candidate hesitated in replies." Respond as promptly and quickly as you can, but do not jump to a hasty, ill-considered answer.

### 11) Do not be peremptory in your answers
A brief answer is proper – but do not fire your answer back. That is a losing game from your point of view. The board member can probably ask questions much faster than you can answer them.

### 12) Do not try to create the answer you think the board member wants
He is interested in what kind of mind you have and how it works – not in playing games. Furthermore, he can usually spot this practice and will actually grade you down on it.

### 13) Do not switch sides in your reply merely to agree with a board member
Frequently, a member will take a contrary position merely to draw you out and to see if you are willing and able to defend your point of view. Do not start a debate, yet do not surrender a good position. If a position is worth taking, it is worth defending.

### 14) Do not be afraid to admit an error in judgment if you are shown to be wrong

The board knows that you are forced to reply without any opportunity for careful consideration. Your answer may be demonstrably wrong. If so, admit it and get on with the interview.

### 15) Do not dwell at length on your present job

The opening question may relate to your present assignment. Answer the question but do not go into an extended discussion. You are being examined for a *new* job, not your present one. As a matter of fact, try to phrase ALL your answers in terms of the job for which you are being examined.

*Basis of Rating*

Probably you will forget most of these "do's" and "don'ts" when you walk into the oral interview room. Even remembering them all will not ensure you a passing grade. Perhaps you did not have the qualifications in the first place. But remembering them will help you to put your best foot forward, without treading on the toes of the board members.

Rumor and popular opinion to the contrary notwithstanding, an oral board wants you to make the best appearance possible. They know you are under pressure – but they also want to see how you respond to it as a guide to what your reaction would be under the pressures of the job you seek. They will be influenced by the degree of poise you display, the personal traits you show and the manner in which you respond.


ABOUT THIS BOOK

This book contains tests divided into Examination Sections. Go through each test, answering every question in the margin. We have also attached a sample answer sheet at the back of the book that can be removed and used. At the end of each test look at the answer key and check your answers. On the ones you got wrong, look at the right answer choice and learn. Do not fill in the answers first. Do not memorize the questions and answers, but understand the answer and principles involved. On your test, the questions will likely be different from the samples. Questions are changed and new ones added. If you understand these past questions you should have success with any changes that arise. Tests may consist of several types of questions. We have additional books on each subject should more study be advisable or necessary for you. Finally, the more you study, the better prepared you will be. This book is intended to be the last thing you study before you walk into the examination room. Prior study of relevant texts is also recommended. NLC publishes some of these in our Fundamental Series. Knowledge and good sense are important factors in passing your exam. Good luck also helps. So now study this Passbook, absorb the material contained within and take that knowledge into the examination. Then do your best to pass that exam.

# EXAMINATION SECTION

# EXAMINATION SECTION
# TEST 1

DIRECTIONS: Each question or incomplete statement is followed by several suggested answers or completions. Select the one that BEST answers the question or completes the statement. *PRINT THE LETTER OF THE CORRECT ANSWER IN THE SPACE AT THE RIGHT.*

1. Assume that the ticket agent at the bathhouse cannot dispense tickets from his machine because of a mechanical failure.
   You should authorize the ticket agent to

   A. sell tickets by hand from the bundle only
   B. stop selling tickets and await the installation of a stand-by machine
   C. collect cash from the patrons and have them escorted through the bathhouse entrance gate
   D. let the patrons deposit admission fees in a box at the bathhouse entrance gate

   1.____

2. If an operator of a four-wheel drive beach buggy leaves the sand portion of a beach and neglects to disengage his forward gears when he starts to drive over area streets to the dump or drop area, he will

   A. cause his transmission to lose linkage
   B. excessively wear his emergency brake
   C. jam up his front differential
   D. seriously damage the springs of the vehicle

   2.____

3. Inventories and replacement of material, supplies, and equipment required for pre-season preparation of beaches is normally scheduled to begin immediately after

   A. April 1st           B. Memorial Day
   C. Labor Day          D. New Year's Day

   3.____

4. On an Emerson Resuscitator, the cylinder is considered full when the cylinder volume indicator shows AT LEAST _____ lbs. pressure per square inch or more.

   A. 900      B. 1300      C. 1800      D. 2800

   4.____

5. The term *deadman,* when used in training courses for lifeguards assigned to oceanfront beaches, refers to

   A. a rope splicing tool
   B. beach cradles
   C. upland anchorage
   D. a fixed warning sign on a stone jetty

   5.____

6. The appropriate arm signal for a lifeguard to give from a standing position on his tower to call for delivery of a resuscitator is:

   A. Pump one arm up and down from an overhead position
   B. Rotary motion in front of chest
   C. Arms extended up -- straight overhead
   D. Arms clasped overhead

   6.____

1

7. The standard technique for executing the back pressure - arm lift method of artificial respiration requires the operator to adhere to a cycle consisting of a prescribed series of motions.
   This cycle should be repeated about _____ times per minute.

   A. two   B. four   C. six   D. twelve

8. Assume that an elderly swimmer has collapsed while swimming. His friend, who is with him, states that the victim has a long history of heart failure. The victim is brought to the first aid station showing signs of shock and labored breathing.
   You should take which one of the following actions?

   A. Apply an oxygen mask tightly to the victim's face
   B. Using the resuscitator, turn on the inhalator valve and apply the face mask
   C. Get him dressed and send him to a hospital with his friend
   D. Wrap him in blankets to keep warm and give him a hot beverage

9. The symptoms of heat prostration MOST usually are:

   A. Face pale, pulse weak; perspiration profuse on forehead, face, and hands; faintness and nausea
   B. Face red, hot, and dry; pulse strong and fast, high fever; perhaps nausea
   C. Face purplish; pulse erratic; feet and hands cold
   D. Face pale; respiration rate down to six; patient violent

10. Of the following, the BEST method for controlling algae growth in outdoor swimming pools is to

    A. treat with heavy dosages of chlorine
    B. raise the pH with additional amounts of calcium carbonate
    C. apply standard rates of copper sulphate
    D. lower the pool level and add fresh water from the main

11. To improve the capabilities of swimming pool filters, a jelly-like substance called a *flock* must be deposited on the surface of the filter bed.
    The flock is formed by adding which of the following two chemicals to the water in the treatment tank?

    A. Anhydrous ammonia and sodium dichromate
    B. Aluminum sulphate and sodium carbonate
    C. Orthotolidine and copper sulphate
    D. Iodides and calcium chloride

12. Pool water returning from the center drain of an outdoor swimming pool is called the

    A. confluent   B. effluent   C. influent   D. affluent

13. Backwashing in a conventional water treatment plant is USUALLY performed by the plant operator when the loss of head reaches _____ pounds per square inch.

    A. 3 1/2-4   B. 5 1/2-7   C. 8-10   D. 11-12

14. Most outdoor swimming pool operations have large heating boilers. These boilers have water columns with look-through water gauges, showing the water level in the boiler. The manual on maintenance and operation of heating plants and auxiliary equipment specifies that, while the boiler is in operation, the water column and gauge glass should be blown down      14._____

    A. daily     B. weekly     C. bi-weekly     D. monthly

15. Conventional gun-type oil burners used at park facilities are required to utilize as fuel     15._____

    A. #2 oil              B. #4 oil
    C. #6 oil              D. a kerosene mixture

16. Chlorine residual in municipally operated pools as required by the department of health shall be kept at NOT LESS THAN _____ ppm.     16._____

    A. 0.01     B. 0.25     C. 0.45     D. 1.0

17. Which of the following should be used to test the pH range (alkaline range) of swimming pool water?     17._____

    A. Ultraviolet light         B. Iodides
    C. Orthotolodine            D. Bromthymol blue

18. The filtration rate per square foot for a conventional filter is _____ gallons per square foot.     18._____

    A. 8     B. 6     C. 5     D. 3

19. Chlorine gas in steel cylinders is used as a sterilant in most outdoor swimming pools. If chlorine gas leaks occur from faulty connections, valve packings, etc., the STANDARD procedure for locating the leaks promptly is to use     19._____

    A. a lighted sulphur taper
    B. a soapy mixture
    C. acetone, applied with a camel hair brush
    D. concentrated ammonia

20. The MOST desirable time to apply lime to fairways on a golf course that is high in the acid range is     20._____

    A. during the rainy season         B. after a long, dry spell
    C. in the fall or spring           D. in late January

21. A bag of commercial fertilizer with a 10-6-4 classification on the printed face of the bag contains which of the following combination of chemicals by weight?     21._____

    A. 10% phosphoric acid, 6% nitrogen, and 4% potash
    B. 10% potash, 6% phosphoric acid, and 4% nitrogen
    C. 10% nitrogen, 6% phosphoric acid, and 4% potash
    D. 10% potash, 6% nitrogen, and 4% phosphoric acid

22. The turf on a tee with 15,000 square feet is badly worn because of traffic density and must be completely rehabilitated. You have completed the step requiring the application of a soil sterilant, and you are ready to apply nitrogen to the soil at a rate of two pounds of available nitrogen per thousand square feet.
    How many 100 pound bags of 10-6-4 fertilizer must be applied to adequately supply the nitrogen requirements?

    A. 10   B. 8   C. 5   D. 3

23. According to regulations relating to lawn-making, which of the following pH ratings of fertilizer is desirable?

    A. 4.5 to 5.0   B. 5.5 to 6.0
    C. 6.5 to 7.0   D. 7.5 to 8.0

24. To facilitate photosynthesis for normal growth, grass should be mowed often enough so that clippings are

    A. equal to mowing height
    B. shorter than mowing height
    C. longer than mowing height
    D. two inches long

25. Of the following, the MOST suitable grass seed mixture for a play field is one containing Kentucky bluegrass and

    A. colonial bent   B. Bermuda grass
    C. zoysia          D. creeping red fescue

26. Red fescue is USUALLY added to a seed mixture because of its

    A. drought resistance   B. fast germination
    C. slow germination     D. coarse texture

27. The four basic procedures generally considered as constituting the minimum maintenance for turf are: (1) selection of adapted grasses; (2) fertilization; (3) watering; and (4)

    A. aerification   B. mowing
    C. plugging       D. rolling

28. The BEST method for improving the soil structure of a heavily compacted playfield is to apply organic top-dressing first and then proceed with

    A. pesticide application   B. mowing and watering
    C. fertilization           D. aerification

29. A fairway should be maintained so that its width averages _____ to _____ feet.

    A. 60; 110   B. 120; 210   C. 220; 260   D. 270; 310

30. A good supplemental program to aid the grass that is already growing and to establish new grass in the thin, worn-out areas of an athletic field is

    A. overseeding   B. rolling
    C. plugging      D. watering

## KEY (CORRECT ANSWERS)

| | | |
|---|---|---|
| 1. A | 11. B | 21. C |
| 2. C | 12. B | 22. D |
| 3. C | 13. B | 23. C |
| 4. C | 14. A | 24. B |
| 5. C | 15. A | 25. D |
| 6. C | 16. D | 26. A |
| 7. D | 17. D | 27. B |
| 8. B | 18. D | 28. D |
| 9. A | 19. D | 29. B |
| 10. C | 20. C | 30. A |

# TEST 2

DIRECTIONS: Each question or incomplete statement is followed by several suggested answers or completions. Select the one that BEST answers the question or completes the statement. *PRINT THE LETTER OF THE CORRECT ANSWER IN THE SPACE AT THE RIGHT.*

1. Traps are customarily surfaced with a layer of sand about _____ inches deep.  1.___

   A. 6  B. 12  C. 18  D. 24

2. A GOOD medium sandy loam for a putting green should contain _____ organic content.  2.___

   A. 5-10%  B. 10-15%  C. 20-30%  D. 30-50%

3. In the maintenance of a putting green, the LEAST necessary piece of equipment is  3.___

   A. putting green mower
   B. power sprayer
   C. aerator
   D. fertilizer spreader

4. The BEST way to maintain a green so that it holds a pitched ball is by  4.___

   A. overwatering
   B. good soil structure
   C. underwatering
   D. high mowing

5. The surface soil on a green should be a medium sandy loam placed _____ to _____ inches deep.  5.___

   A. 2; 4  B. 4; 6  C. 8; 10  D. 12; 18

6. The BEST turf fertilizers today contain about  6.___

   A. 85% slow-release phosphorus
   B. 16% fast-release nitrogen
   C. 50% slow-release nitrogen
   D. 20% phosphorus

7. Since golf course grasses are heavy users of phosphorus, potassium, magnesium, and calcium, the BEST pH range for turf, where maximum quantities of these chemicals are available, is  7.___

   A. 4.2 to 4.8
   B. 5.0 to 5.8
   C. 6.0 to 7.0
   D. 7.2 to 8.2

8. Damage on golf greens and other turf areas caused by the *Fusarium nivale* fungus (snow mold) can BEST be prevented or adequately checked by treatment with  8.___

   A. ammonium methyl arsenates
   B. aluminum sulphate
   C. hydrated lime
   D. cadminates

9. To prevent snow mold, treatment should GENERALLY start  9.___

   A. in early spring
   B. after a heavy rain
   C. in late winter
   D. after a heavy snow

10. Chlordane is used in turf management to

   A. eradicate goose grass
   B. control brown patch
   C. grub-proof soil
   D. stimulate root growth

11. Artificial rinks have refrigerants to cool the brine which is constantly circulated through the wrought-iron pipes imbedded in the floor of the rink.
   The brine can be chilled to below zero degrees Fahrenheit because it contains a chemical salt known as

   A. sodium chloride
   B. calcium chloride
   C. calcium carbonate
   D. ammonium chloride

12. The MINIMUM ice thickness generally considered safe for ice skating on a lake or pond whose depth does not exceed 3 feet is _____ inches.

   A. 2
   B. 3
   C. 5
   D. 6

13. In the operation of an ice skating rink, prior to starting the process of ice building, the slab surface should be painted with _____ paint.

   A. white water
   B. white epoxy
   C. blue water
   D. blue epoxy

14. Crowd control in an ice skating rink includes all phases of the patrons' activities from admissions line-up to the time the patrons leave the rink.
   According to regulations, during special sessions, guards should

   A. skate in a clockwise direction
   B. skate in a counterclockwise direction
   C. be positioned on the ice near the entrances
   D. be positioned off the ice near the entrances

15. When a rink slab has been chilled below freezing temperature, ice can be built to the desired thickness by spraying a fine layer of water onto the slab with a

   A. Toro sprayer
   B. Skinner sprinkler
   C. Rainboni
   D. Zamboni

16. The following is a description of the cooling system of a skating rink: The refrigerant (ammonia or freon) absorbs the heat from the circulating brine which, in turn, lowers the temperature of the skating slab; when the brine is returned to the chiller after leaving the rink floor with absorbed heat, the compressor pumps the refrigerant gases to the condenser.
   The condenser does which of the following?
   It

   A. cools the refrigerant gas to a liquid and returns it to the chiller
   B. heats up the refrigerant gas
   C. transforms the gas into ice crystals
   D. cools the circulating water within the condenser

17. At indoor rinks where atmospheric temperatures remain stable and are not affected by outdoor weather conditions, brine should be circulated at a temperature of APPROXIMATELY _____ degrees Fahrenheit.

   A. 7
   B. 10
   C. 15
   D. 25

18. Conditioning ice surfaces on outdoor rinks in early fall or late spring is BEST accomplished  18.___

    A. after each session
    B. after the sun sets
    C. at 8 A.M.
    D. at 12 noon

19. The standard of thickness for safe skating on lakes and ponds with water depths over three feet is _____ inches.  19.___

    A. two  B. three  C. five  D. seven

20. Assume that a heavy snowstorm has reached the area at the start of the evening session of outdoor rink operations. The one of the following actions that should be taken is to  20.___

    A. send all the skaters home, telling them the rink is closed
    B. let them skate until the snow is too deep to move
    C. cone off one-half of the rink at a time for snow removal operations
    D. give snow shovels to as many skaters as possible and put them to work clearing the rink

21. Of the following trees, the one which is NOT recommended for street tree planting is  21.___

    A. London plane
    B. Gingko
    C. Yellow Pine
    D. Pin Oak

22. Before useful measures can be applied to control a tree disease epidemic in a park, it is FIRST necessary to  22.___

    A. obtain an appropriation for spraying
    B. have a correct diagnosis made of the disease
    C. make an inventory of the diseased trees
    D. wait until winter when the trees are dormant

23. Of the following trees, the one which is generally MOST often recommended for sandy soils is  23.___

    A. American elm
    B. Japanese maple
    C. Chinese poplar
    D. Japanese black pine

24. About 75 percent of all tree diseases, including all mildews, rusts, anthracnoses, and sooty molds, are caused by  24.___

    A. fungi  B. viruses  C. nematodes  D. bacteria

25. Tree crews should be instructed to ALWAYS  25.___

    A. trim the leader of a tree to improve its vitality
    B. prune trees by removing at least 50% of the crowns
    C. remove all injured and diseased wood
    D. fertilize a tree before pruning it

26. Three techniques that you can use to evaluate maintenance activities and determine whether they can be done better are work simplification, work measurement, and

    A. establishment of work performance standards
    B. use of labor saving devices
    C. increased supervision
    D. computerization

27. Staffing is BEST indicated by which of the following activities?

    A. Selection and training of personnel and maintaining favorable conditions of work
    B. Structuring an organization for unity of command, span of control, and lines of authority
    C. Writing task lists for the different titles working at a facility
    D. Working out in broad outline the things that need to be done and the methods for doing them to accomplish the mission of the agency

28. Generally, the MOST practical way to ascertain most readily the number of man-hours it takes to do a job is by

    A. referring to a management analysis handbook
    B. making a detailed analysis of the job
    C. asking the operator performing the job
    D. reviewing job specifications

29. Any violation of the rules or regulations for the government and protection of public parks and property shall be punishable by NOT MORE THAN _____ imprisonment or by a fine of not more than _____ dollars, or by both.

    A. thirty days'; fifty
    B. sixty days'; one hundred
    C. ninety days'; two hundred fifty
    D. one year's; five hundred

30. One workman can hand-rake leaves at the rate of approximately 1,000 square feet in 20 minutes.
    How many men would you assign to a crew to hand rake a grove of trees covering 40,000 square feet in order to accomplish the job within three hours?

    A. 3        B. 30        C. 50        D. 5

# KEY (CORRECT ANSWERS)

| | | | | | |
|---|---|---|---|---|---|
| 1. | A | 11. | B | 21. | C |
| 2. | C | 12. | B | 22. | B |
| 3. | B | 13. | A | 23. | D |
| 4. | B | 14. | D | 24. | A |
| 5. | C | 15. | D | 25. | C |
| 6. | C | 16. | A | 26. | A |
| 7. | C | 17. | C | 27. | A |
| 8. | D | 18. | A | 28. | C |
| 9. | A | 19. | C | 29. | A |
| 10. | C | 20. | C | 30. | D |

# EXAMINATION SECTION
# TEST 1

DIRECTIONS: Each question or incomplete statement is followed by several suggested answers or completions. Select the one that BEST answers the question or completes the statement. *PRINT THE LETTER OF THE CORRECT ANSWER IN THE SPACE AT THE RIGHT.*

1. Assume that a park employee from another district asks you about possible transfers exchanging him and an employee in your district. The two have already discussed it and would like to change.
   For you to DENY such a request is

   A. *advisable;* employees should learn to adjust to their assignments and no one should expect preferential treatment
   B. *inadvisable;* denial may lower work quality and morale when unusual circumstances may be the reason for desiring a change
   C. *inadvisable;* employee requests for transfers always improve work performance of an entire crew
   D. *advisable;* such transfers are never effective and always seem to begin an endless cycle of transfers

   1.____

2. An employee, whom you have reprimanded for low level performance, as begun to work at a level above average.
   For you to PRAISE the employee at least once weekly is a

   A. *good* practice, mainly because the employee will always produce at a higher rate if he know his work is appreciated
   B. *poor* practice, mainly because praise should only be given for an unusually high level of performance
   C. *good* practice, mainly because lack of praise probably caused his low level of performance
   D. *poor* practice, mainly because too much praise seems to lack sincerity

   2.____

3. A laborer reports to you that the park foreman, to whom he is responsible, drinks beer and wine on the job. He states that the foreman's orders are unclear, that he treats his subordinates in an inhumane manner, and he sleeps on the job frequently
   Of the following, the MOST proper action for you to take in this situation is to

   A. tell the employee that you see the foreman every day and he is never intoxicated
   B. ask the employee to keep a secret record of such occurrences and report to you at the end of the month
   C. approach this foreman, along with the laborer who made the complaint, inform him of the allegation, and allow the two to debate the issues
   D. observe this foreman more frequently to discover if the allegation is true and what remedial action need be taken

   3.____

4. You have given a special assignment to an emergency roving work crew to report to a bridge across the horse trail to do some repair work. Of the following, such an order is generally

   4.____

11

A. *good;* the work order permits the general park supervisor to determine exactly the effectiveness of the roving crew
B. *poor;* the work order tells the crew nothing about the nature, equipment, or manpower needed for the repair
C. *good;* roving crews only need to be told where to go and no further details are necessary
D. *poor;* the general park supervisor should not have to tell the roving crew about a repair, since they should know about it first

5. It is one of your responsibilities to schedule the work hours of all the parks employees in your district.
Of the following, for you to discuss a schedule with your subordinate foremen informally before making it final is generally

   A. *undesirable,* since scheduling is your responsibility and you must not let others influence you in carrying it out
   B. *desirable,* since your subordinates are more likely to accept the schedule if they have had some part in its construction
   C. *undesirable,* since too many conflicting ideas will be received which you cannot resolve
   D. *desirable,* since the blame for any errors in the schedule can be spread among several people

6. A supervisor often gives directives in the form of suggestions rather than as formal orders.
This practice is generally

   A. *desirable,* since a series of formal orders may produce resistance from subordinates
   B. *undesirable,* since suggestions would show indecisiveness
   C. *desirable,* since a supervisor should always act in a friendly manner
   D. *undesirable,* since suggestions would not have to be taken seriously

7. Of the following, the BEST statement about the *grapevine* as a form of communication is that it is

   A. *always destructive* of organization since it only carries gossip and false information
   B. *always useful* because it usually provides more accurate information than formal channels of communication
   C. *often useful* because it provides a channel of communication for information which formal lines of communication cannot suitably carry
   D. *never destructive* of organization since it is only used for harmless, idle gossip

8. The manner in which a supervisor directs his workers usually influences the amount of work which the workers do.
Of the following, workers are MOST likely to produce more work under a supervisor who assigns a job,

   A. instructs in detail how the job is to be done, and closely watches that the job is performed in that way
   B. and leaves it to the workers to figure out how the job is to be done, and checks up only when the job is finished

C. instructs in detail how the job is to be done, and checks the work only when the job is finished
D. leaves the workers to perform it as he has trained them to, and checks occasionally to see that the job is being performed adequately

9. An essential piece of equipment has developed a serious mechanical problem. It can be operated in a limited manner, but will eventually have to go to the district shop for a few weeks for major repairs. Before deciding whether you will have the machine repaired at once or use it as it is for a while, you wish to confer with your foremen. Two of your foremen, however, are new and inexperienced.
Of the following, the BEST statement about including them in the meeting is that such action is generally

   A. *desirable,* since such a meeting will give the men a change from their ordinary work
   B. *undesirable,* since these inexperienced men can contribute nothing and would be just wasting time
   C. *desirable,* since such a meeting with experienced men provides these inexperienced men with an opportunity to learn
   D. *undesirable,* since any ideas offered by these inexperienced men can only confuse the meeting

10. The maintenance of good employee morale is important to high production.
The existence of legitimate grievance channels through which an employee may effectively express dissatisfaction normally tends, in the long run, to _____ the number of grievances.

   A. *raise* morale while *diminishing*
   B. *lower* morale while *Increasing*
   C. *have no effect* on morale or
   D. *raise* morale while *increasing*

11. While making your rounds in the district, you find that one of your men is making a mistake which is clearly due to negligence on his part.
Of the following, your BEST course of action normally is to

   A. reprimand the man at once, loudly, so that other employees in the area will know that you will not tolerate such mistakes
   B. talk to the man privately, letting him know in strong terms that you are personally very angry with him for such performance since it reflects on your superiors' view of you
   C. reprimand the man, then, for several days after, remind him that you are checking his performance so that he will not repeat his negligence
   D. use the situation to train the employee in proper procedure and point out to him the bad effects of negligent work

12. A laborer with an otherwise good work history often comes in late. You ask him why, and he answers, *I just can't get up in the morning. Frankly, I've just lost interest in the job; when I do get up, I've got to rush like crazy to get here.*
Which of the following responses from you would MOST likely lead to a constructive solution of the problem?

A. You don't know what an alarm clock is?
B. Are you having problems with your family?
C. Why have you lost interest in the job?
D. Well, that's no reason for coming in late.

13. A worker over 50 will generally be better than a worker under 25 in all of the following areas EXCEPT

    A. frequency of absences
    B. length of sick-leave absences
    C. safety record
    D. number of grievances

14. Of the following, the advantage for a supervisor in delegating his authority is that such delegation normally provides him with a means to

    A. devote his own time to the more important aspects of a job and assign the less important aspects to his subordinates
    B. keep close personal control over all details in his district
    C. restrict a subordinate's freedom to make wrong decisions
    D. earn his subordinates' respect by working alongside them at the same job

15. In preparing general assignments and work schedules of a group of employees, a supervisor can generally expect the BEST results by making assignments according to which one of the following?

    A. A method which always places workers with similar skills together
    B. A method which takes into account the personalities of the group members
    C. Group preference, which will usually lead to high quality output
    D. A method which does not involve personality factors

16. Workers separated by great distances from the source of authority at the top of the organization have difficulty in *communicating upward.*
Upward communication MOST NEARLY means

    A. directives that originate with top officials
    B. messages relayed from lower levels to management
    C. communication among workers
    D. a worker's ability to understand formally written orders

17. An angry public works employee tells you about a vending machine concessionaire who has thrown his litter onto the area recently cleaned by the employee. Upon investigation, you discover that the wastebaskets provided for the concessionaire, for which the worker is responsible, are filled to capacity.
Of the following, the BEST course for you to take in this situation is to

    A. tell the employee that his failure to perform his work is the cause of the trouble; he must improve immediately or be fired
    B. call attention to the employee's poor work record and tell him that he has caused you personal embarrassment
    C. console the employee, tell him that the vendor or another employee is at fault
    D. tell the employee that he should be sure the baskets are properly emptied and if he performs his work correctly, such problems will be eliminated

18. The efficiency of an employee depends in part on the type and quality of training he receives.
Of the following, the BEST method for you to use to train new laborers during a period when personnel is short is to train them

    A. only for the immediate job operation
    B. for more than one operation only if they had prior experience
    C. on a continuous basis so that immediate and long-range job operations are considered
    D. by giving all the details of the job operation during the first training session

18.____

19. A park foreman has indicated to you that a major steel connector on a basketball court in the district needs to be replaced. You then later discover that the extent of the damage on the court requires the removal of the damaged connector immediately.
Of the following, the BEST way to have the connector replaced is for you to report the situation first to the

    A. roving work crew who is directly responsible for all emergencies
    B. regular work crew who is directly responsible for the area
    C. mechanical shop who will replace the connector
    D. senior supervisor of park operations who is directly responsible for property damage

19.____

20. Assume that you were told of a minor incident involving one of the workers and a teenage boy in the park. The following day, you overhear the true details of the incident which were much more serious than those which you were told.
Why is it that information originating at the lowest level of an organization often reaches higher levels in a completely different form?

    A. Workers at the lowest levels in an organization usually enjoy deceiving their superiors.
    B. Workers often feel that supervisors are their enemy and, therefore, they prefer to keep any information about themselves within their own ranks.
    C. Information starting at the lower levels tends to be stripped of details which might anger or upset the immediate supervisor.
    D. Most supervisors are too busy to be hindered by disciplinary reports about their workers.

20.____

21. While he is preparing for a rock concert expected to draw a capacity crowd, an employee scheduled to assist with the affair is injured. From past experience, you know that Bill is the best replacement for the injured employee.
Of the following, the MOST appropriate action for you to take is to

    A. approach Bill as you would any friend, pointing out your faith in him
    B. tell Bill that you know that someone else is available, but that he is so fussy that you'd rather have him, since he always knows what to do
    C. give Bill an order stating that he will replace the injured employee
    D. tell Bill what has happened so that he understands why he is being asked to work and make him feel that he has a part in an important decision

21.____

22. Following a two-month period of regular inspection procedures and a number of discussions with the foreman and individual laborers about proper maintenance procedures, you still receive complaints from patrons about substandard maintenance of the area adjacent to a swimming pool in your district.
The one of the following which is the MOST appropriate action for you to take is to

   A. hold private sessions with each laborer to find out how to correct the situation
   B. hold a group conference to express your dissatisfaction in clear terms and to give the work crew a chance to present their side of the issue
   C. complain to your superiors to get help concerning the best method of improvement
   D. hold a group conference, calling only upon members of the crew who have performed satisfactorily for improvement ideas

23. Assume that you want to train a new park foreman by rotating him to all blotter stops in your district so he will receive on-the-job training from experienced park foremen. You also plan to hold daily sessions with the new foreman.
Of the following, the MOST correct statement about this procedure is that it is generally

   A. *undesirable;* the new foreman would not know what to do with so many people directing him
   B. *desirable;* a person in the same job position as the new employee would always be helpful
   C. *desirable;* the new foreman would receive varied and needed experience along with supervisory attention
   D. *undesirable;* a person in the same job position always resents new persons and does not properly train them

24. An employee complains to you about what he feels is the overbearing conduct of the park foreman who is his superior.
Of the following, the MOST immediate action that you should generally take is to

   A. reprimand the foreman immediately and demand that he adhere to a more democratic method of supervision
   B. investigate the situation since an employee usually does not find it easy to complain about his superior
   C. dismiss the allegation since most employees enjoy creating problems for others, especially for their superiors
   D. defend the foreman, reminding the employee that the foreman has the proper knowledge and experience to handle his position efficiently

25. During the past three weeks, Frank Parker, usually an efficient employee, has developed an unusual attitude and frequently *pops off* in the presence of other workers. His work performance has fallen below the accepted standard and his attitude has lowered the morale of his work team.
Of the following, the BEST action for you to take is to

   A. reprimand Frank by reminding him that neither his attitude nor his poor work will be tolerated
   B. call Frank in for a conference to discuss his work performance
   C. ignore Frank's behavior, since he has performed well in the past
   D. transfer Frank to other work locations at set intervals, to keep his morale and work standards up

## KEY (CORRECT ANSWERS)

1. B
2. D
3. D
4. B
5. B

6. A
7. C
8. D
9. C
10. A

11. D
12. C
13. B
14. A
15. B

16. B
17. D
18. C
19. C
20. C

21. D
22. B
23. C
24. B
25. B

# TEST 2

DIRECTIONS: Each question or incomplete statement is followed by several suggested answers or completions. Select the one that BEST answers the question or completes the statement. *PRINT THE LETTER OF THE CORRECT ANSWER IN THE SPACE AT THE RIGHT.*

1. Which of the following is the MOST likely action a supervisor should take to help establish an effective working relationship with his departmental superiors?

    A. Delay the implementation of new procedures received from superiors in order to evaluate their appropriateness
    B. Skip the chain of command whenever he feels that it is to his advantage
    C. Keep supervisors informed of problems in his area and the steps taken to correct them
    D. Don't take up superiors' time by discussing anticipated problems but wait until the difficulties occur

2. Of the following, the action a supervisor could take which would generally be MOST conducive to the establishment of an effective working relationship with employees includes

    A. maintaining impersonal relationships to prevent development of biased actions
    B. treating all employees equally without adjusting for individual differences
    C. continuous observation of employees on the job with insistence on constant improvement
    D. careful planning and scheduling of work for your employees

3. Which of the following procedures is the LEAST likely to establish effective working relationships between employees and supervisors?

    A. Encouraging *two-way* communication with employees
    B. Periodic discussion with employees regarding their job performance
    C. Ignoring employees' gripes concerning job difficulties
    D. Avoiding personal prejudices in dealing with employees

4. Criticism can be used as a tool to point out the weak areas of a subordinate's work performance.
   Of the following, the BEST action for a supervisor to take so that his criticism will be accepted is to

    A. focus his criticism on the act instead of on the person
    B. exaggerate the errors in order to motivate the employee to do better
    C. pass judgment quickly and privately, without investigating the circumstances of the error
    D. generalize the criticism and not specifically point out the errors in performance

5. Assume that it has come to your attention that two of your subordinates have shouted at each other and have almost engaged in a fist fight; luckily, they were separated by some of the other employees.
   Of the following, your BEST immediate course of action would generally be to

A. reprimand the senior of the two subordinates, since he should have known better
B. hear the story from both employees and any witnesses and then take needed disciplinary action
C. ignore the matter, since nobody was physically hurt
D. immediately suspend and fine both employees pending a departmental hearing

6. You have been delegating some of your authority to one of your subordinates because of his leadership potential.
Which of the following actions is LEAST conducive to the growth and development of this individual for a supervisory position?

   A. Use praise only when it will be effective
   B. Give very detailed instructions and supervise the employee closely to be sure that the instructions are followed precisely
   C. Let the subordinate proceed with his planned course of action even if mistakes, within a permissible range, are made
   D. Intervene on behalf of the subordinate whenever an assignment becomes difficult for him

7. A rumor has been spreading in your department concerning the possibility of layoffs due to decreased revenues.
As a supervisor, you should generally

   A. deny the rumor, whether it is true or false, in order to keep morale from declining
   B. inform the men to the best of your knowledge about this situation and keep them advised of any new information
   C. tell the men to forget about the rumor and concentrate on increasing their productivity
   D. ignore the rumor, since it is not authorized information

8. Within an organization, every supervisor should know to whom he reports and who reports to him.
The one of the following which is achieved by use of such structured relationships is

   A. unity of command           B. confidentiality
   C. esprit de corps            D. promotion opportunities

9. While observing a summer aide perform his duties, you notice that he is using many useless motions in completing a task.
In order to improve the productivity of the aid, you generally can BEST use this opportunity to

   A. reprimand the aide for his inefficient performance
   B. point out the aide's inefficiency and compare this performance to other mistakes he has committed, in order to motivate him
   C. provide training for the aide at this time in order to increase his future work productivity
   D. let the aide learn by doing

10. While spot-checking the activities of summer park aides, you notice a few of them engaging in *horseplay*.
Of the following, the MOST appropriate action for you to take would be to

A. tell the summer park aides to immediately stop the *horseplay* and continue with their work
B. ignore their actions if their work is progressing satisfactorily; after all, *horseplay* is normal among youthful employees
C. reprimand the aides by telling them to go home for the day
D. report this incident to the aides' immediate supervisor when you see him

11. Of the following, the action of a supervisor that would be LEAST likely to give the general public a favorable impression of the parks department would be to

    A. provide information concerning the department's interest in community affairs
    B. acquaint friends and others with departmental activities that provide a favorable view of the department
    C. speak unfavorably of the working conditions established by the department
    D. participate in and support civic and community activities

12. Assume that it has come to your attention that small amounts of minor park supplies and materials have been disappearing.
    Of the following, the BEST statement about ignoring this situation is that to do so is

    A. *desirable;* since no large thefts have occurred, it would be better to forget about the little items
    B. *desirable;* since the work is being done, there is no reason to upset the workers
    C. *undesirable;* the park may have to close due to the thefts of supplies
    D. *undesirable;* you would be condoning such acts unless you take immediate steps to curtail these occurrences

13. Several members of a work crew have approached you with the idea of rotating men on job assignments such as raking leaves, picking up paper, and making minor repairs on the tennis courts.
    Of the following, your BEST answer would be:

    A. I'm sorry, but such a change would make it impossible to keep track of who does what
    B. If you all agree to the change, let's try it
    C. I'm not sure if that is allowed. I'll send in some papers and notify you in a couple of weeks
    D. The work is getting done now. Leave things as they are

14. Which of the following is generally the MOST effective way for you to communicate information to the workers?

    A. Face-to-face communication
    B. A notice on the bulletin board
    C. The telephone
    D. A messenger with a memo

15. While walking through the playground, you find one of the workers sitting on a park bench. He has done an excellent job of cleaning the area; and when you approach him, he says that he is *just taking a short break.*
    Of the following, the MOST acceptable course of action for you to take in this situation is to

A. tell him there is plenty of work still to be done
B. tell him to save his rests for lunch breaks
C. pretend that you don't see him
D. tell him that he is entitled to a quick break because he has done a good job, but to make it a small break

16. Assume that you have found out that one of the workers usually drinks alcohol heavily on his lunch hour.
Of the following, the BEST course of action for you to take in such a situation is to

A. try to isolate him so that he will not influence the other workers
B. call his wife and ask her for her help
C. tactfully suggest that he seek professional help
D. try to find the cause of his problem and help him solve it

16.____

17. Penetrating oil is OFTEN used for

A. cutting pipe
B. loosening rusted bolts
C. clearing clogged pipes
D. lubricating electric appliances

17.____

18. Sweating or condensation of moisture on the outside of a pipe is MOST likely to occur on _____ pipes.

A. hot water
C. cold water
B. steam
D. compressed air

18.____

19. Turpentine may be used as a thinner for

A. shellac
C. calcimine
B. latex paints
D. oil paints

19.____

20. Creosote is COMMONLY used to

A. preserve wood from rot
B. fireproof wood structures
C. change the color of wood
D. hasten the seasoning of wood

20.____

21. The MOST commonly used welding torches are fed by two tanks of gas.
One of these tanks holds acetylene and the other holds

A. carbon dioxide
C. nitrogen
B. hydrogen
D. oxygen

21.____

22. When 8-32 is used to designate a screw, the figures represent, respectively,

A. threads/inch and diameter
B. length and diameter
C. diameter and length
D. diameter and threads/inch

22.____

23. Galvanized pipe has a finish coating of

A. lead
B. zinc
C. copper
D. nickel

23.____

24. It is not considered good practice to paint portable wooden ladders. Of the following, the MOST logical reason for this is that the

    A. painted rungs would become slippery when wet
    B. paint might rub off on a supporting wall
    C. paint might hide serious defects
    D. paint would quickly wear off

25. The type of fastener MOST commonly used when bolting to concrete uses a(n)

    A. expansion shield      B. U-bolt
    C. toggle bolt      D. turnbuckle

---

# KEY (CORRECT ANSWERS)

1. C      11. C
2. D      12. D
3. C      13. B
4. A      14. A
5. B      15. D

6. B      16. C
7. B      17. B
8. A      18. C
9. C      19. D
10. A      20. A

21. D
22. D
23. B
24. C
25. A

# EXAMINATION SECTION
# TEST 1

DIRECTIONS: Each question or incomplete statement is followed by several suggested answers or completions. Select the one that BEST answers the question or completes the statement. *PRINT THE LETTER OF THE CORRECT ANSWER IN THE SPACE AT THE RIGHT.*

1. To cut a number of 2" x 4" lengths of wood accurately at an angle of 45°, it is BEST to use a  1.____

    A. coping saw            B. mitre-box
    C. square                D. marking gauge

2. The leverage that can be obtained with a wrench is determined MAINLY by the  2.____

    A. material of which the wrench is made
    B. gripping surface of the jaw
    C. length of the handle
    D. thickness of the wrench

3. Many electric power tools, such as drills, have a third conductor in the line cord which should be connected to a grounded part of the power receptacle.
The reason for this is to  3.____

    A. have a spare wire in case one power wire should break
    B. strengthen the power lead so that it cannot be easily damaged
    C. protect the user of the tool from electric shocks
    D. allow use of the tool for extended periods of time without overheating

4. A cold chisel whose head has become *mushroomed* should NOT be used primarily because  4.____

    A. it is impossible to hit the head squarely
    B. the chisel will not cut accurately
    C. chips might fly from the head
    D. the chisel has lost its *temper*

5. Catch basins are used in connection with  5.____

    A. buried gas mains
    B. underground springs
    C. storm water sewer systems
    D. water heaters

6. The ratio of air to gasoline in an automobile engine is controlled by the  6.____

    A. gas filter            B. fuel pump
    C. carburetor            D. distributor

7. Which of the following trees recommended for street planting has been greatly over-used?  7.____

    A. London Plane          B. Flowering Japanese Cherry
    C. Dawn Redwood          D. Red Oak

8. Generally, during dry weather, a clay tennis court should be

   A. wet down at the end of each day's play, then well rolled early the next morning
   B. well rolled at the end of each day's play, then wet down early the next morning
   C. wet down and well rolled at the end of each day's play
   D. wet down and well rolled early each morning before play

9. The playing surface of a clay tennis court *generally* consists of

   A. silt
   B. clay, silt, and sand
   C. clay and silt
   D. silt and sand

10. Of the following, the frequency with which revenues from beaches, swimming pools, golf courses, and ice skating rinks are *normally* prepared for deposit is

    A. twice daily
    B. daily
    C. twice a week
    D. weekly

11. The one of the following which is the BEST time, as a general rule, for removing debris deposited on the beaches by the tide during the winter is

    A. every day
    B. once a week
    C. once a month
    D. only before the opening of the beaches for the summer

12. Snow fences are usually used at beaches in winter PRIMARILY to

    A. prevent snow from drifting too high near buildings
    B. prevent driftwood from coming too far up on the beaches
    C. control wind erosion of sand from the beaches
    D. temporarily replace regular fences and railings which are damaged

13. Of the following, the filter material used in all of the gravity system filters of public swimming pools is

    A. sand
    B. diatomaceous earth
    C. anthrafilt
    D. resin-impregnated paper

14. At an outdoor public rink, the PROPER procedure during a snowfall *normally* is to

    A. close half the rink at a time for snow removal, leaving the other half open for skating
    B. disregard the snow until the normal end of sessions, at which time snow should be removed and ice renovated
    C. close the rink, as snow usually creates hazardous skating conditions
    D. clear the rink, then melt the snow with a hot-water spray; skating may be resumed when the water freezes

15. If ice expands or contracts because of temperature fluctuations, large fissures or cracks can form. Such cracks *generally* are

    A. *abnormal* and an indication of thin ice conditions
    B. *normal,* but can become trip hazards, and so should be filled in
    C. *normal* and safe, and can be ignored
    D. *very common,* and the best indication of thin ice

16. According to instructions, the FIRST and MOST important duty performed each morning by every greensman at a golf course is to _____ the greens.  16.____

    A. water  B. mow  C. rake  D. whip

17. A golfer is entitled to tee off and must be ready to tee off when his number is called by the starter.  17.____
    Golfers not present or ready to tee off when their number is called will, upon returning to the starter's board, be reassigned by the starter _____ numbers below the number

    A. 10; on their ticket
    B. 10; being called at the time of their return
    C. 20; on their ticket
    D. 20; being called at the time of their return

18. Assume that a player is at a public golf course which is not a pitch-putt course, and that this golfer does not have an approved adjustable club.  18.____
    Of the following, the equipment that this player MUST have is

    A. at least three golf clubs, including a putter and one wood
    B. at least seven golf clubs, including a putter and one wood
    C. a golf bag or carrier and at least three golf clubs, one of which must be a putter
    D. a golf bar or carrier and at least seven golf clubs, including a putter and one wood

19. Ball marks on golf course greens must be repaired as they occur.  19.____
    To repair such marks before they dry out, each greensman must be equipped with a

    A. sharp table fork or penknife
    B. bamboo or wooden rake
    C. spade
    D. watering can

20. Performance of necessary maintenance on machines according to a regular schedule is generally  20.____

    A. *desirable,* primarily because the appearance of machinery should be kept up
    B. *undesirable,* primarily because it is a waste of both man-hours and machine-hours to repair functioning machinery
    C. *undesirable,* primarily because too much maintenance is as bad as not enough
    D. *desirable,* primarily because regularly maintained machinery is more efficient and less likely to suffer a major breakdown at a time when it is urgently needed

21. During your regular inspection tour, you notice a youth writing on a statue.  21.____
    Of the following, the BEST immediate action for long-range results is for you to

    A. ignore the youth, because if you indicate to him that he is wrong, he will only continue to write
    B. approach the youth and inform him that you will take him to police headquarters for breaking park department rules
    C. tell the youth that you know he has defaced property throughout the park and is prohibited by law from entering the park again
    D. talk to the youth concerning the cost of graffiti, give him a sincere but stern warning on the penalties involved, and suggest that he join a *neighborhood task force*

22. An irate citizen telephones you to state her anger about a parks department employee. She states that the employee has asked her children not to pick shrubs or flowers and the children were heartbroken because they were making a bouquet for their grandmother. The mother states that the park is for the enjoyment of the public and such action by the employee was unwarranted.
Of the following, the BEST method of handling the situation is for you to

    A. apologize for the employee by informing the citizen that he was new and did not understand children
    B. inform the caller that she will have to file a written complaint to the parks department
    C. sympathize with the caller, but tell her that park rules prohibit such action because it marks the beauty of the park
    D. tell the caller that park employees are properly trained, and always perform correctly

23. After repeated warnings by you about violation of parks department regulations, two concessionaries have had their permits revoked. The two wish to be reinstated and have asked local community groups to intervene. The groups, concerned with protecting the rights of the citizens against unwarranted actions, have come to you asking for the reasons for the revocations and for all information related to them.
Of the following, the BEST course of action for you to take for the maintenance of good public relations is to

    A. state that information concerning internal operations is confidential
    B. provide the information requested, avoiding opinions and off-the-record comments
    C. inform the groups that you do not know the reasons for the permit revocations, but you will inform them as soon as the information becomes available
    D. explain that standards are set for concessionaires and any departure from these regulations is cause for revocation

24. Assume that as a newly appointed supervisor, one of the first work orders you issue involves painting and restoring equipment in a little-used children's play area in a district park.
The one of the following which would be the MOST likely effect upon patrons who frequent such areas is that this would

    A. create better public relations, since a pleasing appearance of physical facilities helps establish confidence in the park system
    B. have no effect on public relations since the area was not often used
    C. create poor public relations since such repairs will require closing the area
    D. raise suspicions concerning the park's efficiency, since it was senseless to improve a little-used play area

25. In order to get maximum use of facilities adjacent to an outdoor pool, you have decided to open the pavilions as winter recreation centers for indoor games.
Of the following, the MOST important factor for the effectiveness of such a program is generally

    A. how well the immediate director is known and liked
    B. the amount of publicity news media give the program
    C. how well similar park programs have been accepted by the public
    D. how well the public understands and cooperates with the program

## KEY (CORRECT ANSWERS)

1. B
2. C
3. C
4. C
5. C

6. C
7. A
8. A
9. B
10. B

11. A
12. C
13. C
14. A
15. B

16. D
17. D
18. C
19. A
20. D

21. C
22. B
23. C
24. A
25. C

# TEST 2

DIRECTIONS: Each question or incomplete statement is followed by several suggested answers or completions. Select the one that BEST answers the question or completes the statement. *PRINT THE LETTER OF THE CORRECT ANSWER IN THE SPACE AT THE RIGHT.*

1. Assume that two very powerful community groups, who have both been very cooperative with park programs, are in disagreement concerning dogs in the park. One group insists that park rules prohibit unleashed dogs, while the other asserts that the rule has never been enforced. Of the following, the BEST course of action for you to take in order to maintain good public relations is to

    A. inform both groups that a special area of the park will be set aside for unleashed dogs
    B. tell both groups that they will have to file written complaints before any action can be taken
    C. tell the group desirous of unleashed dogs that park rules prohibit unleashed animals, but appeals for change may be made
    D. inform the group protesting unleashed dogs that, since the rules has not been strictly enforced in the past, it would be fruitless to try now

2. Assume that you are meeting with the cabinet of the local office of neighborhood government. These community representatives complain that a certain playground has been repeatedly vandalized. Your men have made repairs at this facility on several occasions. Of the following, the MOST effective advice you can give the cabinet about such a situation generally is that

    A. you are short-handed and nothing more can be done
    B. the community has a large responsibility for seeing that park facilities are not vandalized, and suggest that a community group accept responsibility for reporting all vandalism to the police
    C. the cabinet members should write a letter to the mayor
    D. the cabinet should not interfere in the administration of the parks; the parks department is best able to determine how to handle a situation involving vandalism

3. As a supervisor, you may speak to various groups or organizations about services and activities provided by the district.
   Of the following, the factor normally LEAST necessary for making a successful talk is

    A. a good idea or subject for discussion
    B. useful knowledge of your subject
    C. formal training in the techniques of public speaking
    D. a sincere desire and basic ability to express your ideas

4. You have received a letter of complaint from a local resident that a laborer in a playground in the district was rude to her and her children. You have received other complaints about this person in the past.
   In the interest of maintaining good community relations, the one of the following actions which it would normally be BEST for you to take is to

A. investigate, and promptly telephone or write an appropriate response describing what action, if any, you have taken and send a report to the local office
B. investigate, and send a report to the local office to let the local office decide if any action is appropriate
C. dismiss the letter as the work of a chronic crank and do nothing; to investigate might annoy your man
D. file the complaint so that if several similar ones come in, you can take appropriate action in the future

5. Which of the following is MOST likely to project an unfavorable impression of a municipal agency?
If you are

   A. making a telephone call, identify yourself and the organization immediately
   B. dealing with the public, try to make the people feel important
   C. making a visit, do not hesitate to leave your car improperly parked
   D. delivering supplies, obey the speed limit and stay in the right lane when not passing

6. Of the following, two factors upon which good public relations for a municipal agency depend are favorable media coverage and generally

   A. a good service performance record
   B. the scope of services to be provided
   C. the magnitude of the annual budget
   D. the type of equipment used

7. Several groups interested in determining a location for the new baseball diamond have presented their preferences to you. Rather than yield to the loudest group, you have asked the interested groups to make their requests based on facts such as size, accessibility, number of trees that would have to be destroyed, etc.
Of the following, the BEST reason for making your decision based on these factors is that

   A. facts are always easy to obtain
   B. the decision has a basis which can be defended by interested parties
   C. by this method, the loudest group doesn't always win
   D. you can never go wrong by using facts

8. If a person who is using a park facility is treated discourteously by a park employee, the offended person is *generally* likely to think ill of

   A. just that employee
   B. just that employee and his supervisor
   C. the parks department and the city or county
   D. just the park where the incident took place

9. If a member of the public is seen violating one of the park rules and regulations, the BEST way to stop the person from continuing is generally to

A. shout loudly at the person, so that he and all others who have seen him will know that his actions violate park rules
B. approach the person courteously, tell him of his violation, and be willing to answer any question he may have about the rules
C. inform the person that he is in violation of the rules and must leave the park facilities at once
D. ignore the violation, since park personnel do not want the reputation of acting like policemen

10. Park rules and regulations exist to insure that the greatest number of people make the best use of park facilities. Of the following, the responsibility for seeing that the public follows the rules and regulations falls PRIMARILY on

    A. the supervisor alone, since he is usually the highest ranking person
    B. both the supervisor and the park foreman, since they are supervisory personnel
    C. all park employees who have contact with the public
    D. parks department administrators since they are the ones who establish park priorities

11. The one of the following requirements which is usually necessary for signs to be effective in informing the public of a park regulation is that

    A. the bottom of signs be no more than 4 1/2 feet from the ground
    B. there be as many of the same type of sign as possible
    C. the signs be legibly lettered, with correct spelling and wording
    D. the signs be distributed at random around the park facility

12. If a lifeguard at a public beach or pool gives one long blast on his whistle, he is

    A. signaling that he is leaving his station in response to an emergency situation
    B. calling the attention of the public to violations of rules and regulations
    C. calling for the attention of the lifeguard chief or lieutenant (not an emergency)
    D. signaling that he is going off duty, and another lifeguard should cover his station

13. The one of the following conditions which is LEAST necessary to insure that the public uses rubbish baskets is that the baskets be

    A. in good physical condition
    B. emptied when full
    C. conspicuously located
    D. distributed randomly throughout the park area

14. If a park facility is kept clean and well-maintained, the rate of vandlism will likely

    A. *be lowered,* since public cooperation is induced by well-kept facilities
    B. *be raised,* since vandals prefer to damage a well-kept area
    C. *remain the same,* since the upkeep of a facility has no effect on the rate of vandalism
    D. *be raised,* since a well-kept facility is easier to damage than a poorly-kept facility

15. In addition to planned regular maintenance, the one of the following which is the best way to keep park facilities at a high level of operating efficiency so the public may have the GREATEST use of the facilities is usually to

   A. make frequent and thorough inspections of all facilities followed by corrective measures when needed
   B. wait for complaints from park facility users since manpower is wasted by correcting defects normally unnoticed by the public
   C. take corrective action only on complaints made to the borough offices, since only these need be considered serious
   D. disregard most complaints, since regular maintenance corrects all serious defects in park facilities

15._____

Directions 16-25.

DIRECTIONS: Questions 16 through 25 are to be answered on the basis of the information given below and the two tables which follow. Some of the questions require taking into consideration the information in one or both of the two tables and in the following paragraphs. No question relates to a previous question.

As a General Park Foreman, R. Carson has been newly assigned to Undulant Memorial Park, District 841. The schedules have been made up by the previous General Park Foreman for the week of June 30 to July 6. The park has 500 acres of grass, a wooded picnic area of 200 acres, 4 comfort stations, a surfaced playground area for children, 10 tennis courts, 2 baseball diamonds, 4 softball diamonds, 6 basketball courts, and 100 acres of additional wooded area which are being converted to picnic grounds. The conversion of the wooded area is to be completed before July 4th.

The roster of personnel assigned to District 841 includes 1 General Park Foreman, 2 Park Foremen, 9 laborers, 4 attendants (whose activities are restricted to the tennis courts and locker rooms), and 12 seasonal park helpers. The equipment assigned to District 841 includes 1 pickup truck, 1 dump truck, 1 tractor and grass cutting attachment, 2 Toro mowers, and 2 hand mowers.

The operating requirements (weekly scheduled operations which must be met) for District 841 include a daily morning garbage pickup for the picnic area, a twice weekly pickup Monday and Friday for the rest of the District, and a weekly walking pickup of the entire area on Thursday (see Table II). A garbage pickup of the picnic area takes 4 hours and requires the use of 3 men and a dump truck. The garbage pickup for the rest of the district requires the use of that crew for an additional 3 hours. The walking pickup takes 8 hours and requires the use of 6 men and a pickup truck.

The hours of operation for all facilities in District 841 are 8 A.M. to 9 P.M. Seasonal park helpers are scheduled to work 6 days per week, and employees in all other titles are scheduled to work 5 days per week. One hour is given for lunch or supper.

## TABLE I

TIME SCHEDULE     Periods:     From June 23 to June 29
Dept. of Parks     Park:     Undulant Memorial Park
District 841

| Title | Sat. 6/23 | Sun. 6/24 | Mon. 6/25 | Tues. 6/26 | Wed. 6/27 | Thurs. 6/28 | Fri. 6/29 |
|---|---|---|---|---|---|---|---|
| General Park Foreman | 8-5 | 8-5 | 8-5 | 8-5 | 8-5 | | |
| Park Foreman | | 8-5 | 8-5 | 8-5 | | 8-5 | 8-5 |
| Park Foreman | 1-9 | | 1-9 | | 1-9 | 1-9 | 1-9 |
| Laborers 3* | 8-5 | | | 8-5 | 8-5 | 8-5 | 8-5 |
| Laborers 3 | | 8-5 | 8-5 | 8-5 | 8-5 | 8-5 | |
| Laborers 3 | 1-9 | | 1-9 | | 1-9 | 1-9 | 1-9 |
| Seasonal Park Helper 3 | 8-5 | | 8-5 | 8-5 | 8-5 | 8-5 | 8-5 |
| Seasonal Park Helper 3 | | 8-5 | 8-5 | 8-5 | 8-5 | 8-5 | 8-5 |
| Seasonal Park Helper 3 | 1-9 | | 1-9 | 1-9 | 1-9 | 1-9 | 1-9 |
| Seasonal Park Helper 3 | | 1-9 | 1-9 | 1-9 | 1-9 | 1-9 | 1-9 |
| Attendant 2 | 10-6 | 10-6 | 10-6 | 10-6 | 10-6 | | |
| Attendant 2 | 10-6 | 10-6 | | | 10-6 | 10-6 | 10-6 |

### LEGEND
*Number of employees in that title on that time schedule
8-5 Tour of duty from 8 A.M. to 5 P.M. (8-hour shift)
1-9 Tour of duty from 1 P.M. to 9 P.M. (7-hour shift)
10-6 Tour of duty from 10 A.M. to 6 P.M. (7-hour shift)

## TABLE II

### OPERATING REQUIREMENTS

EQUIPMENT

| | Sat. 6/23 | Sun. 6/24 | Mon. 6/25 | Tues. 6/26 | Wed. 6/27 | Thurs. 6/28 | Fri. 6/29 |
|---|---|---|---|---|---|---|---|
| Pickup Truck | | | | | | 6 / 8 | |
| Dump Truck | 3 / 4 | 3 / 4 | 3 / 7 | 3 / 4 | 3 / 4 | 3 / 4 | 3 / 7 … 3 |

### LEGEND

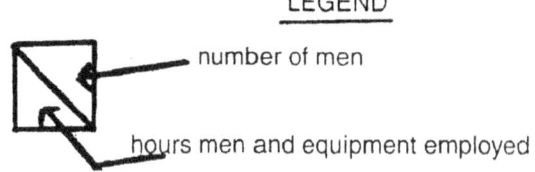
number of men
hours men and equipment employed

16. A man using the tractor with grass-cutting equipment can cut an average of ten acres of grass per hour; with a Toro mower, 4 acres per hour; and with a hand mower, 1 acre per hour. Only 250 of the 500 acres of grass can be cut with the tractor.
    The total number of man-hours (one man-hour is defined as one hour of work for one man) it will take to cut all 500 acres of grass using all the available machinery simultaneously is MOST NEARLY

    A. 50   B. 100   C. 125   D. 200

17. The conversion of the wooded area to picnic grounds is complete except for the installation of 100 additional picnic tables. It is estimated that this project requires the use of a pickup truck and 2 men for 40 hours. Because this is a priority item, it will be worked on during all the hours the park is open.
    If the project must be completed by Friday noon for the 4th of July holiday, considering that the operating requirements listed in Table II must be met, we would expect the project to begin

    A. Saturday afternoon    B. Sunday morning
    C. Monday afternoon      D. Tuesday afternoon

18. Assuming that all the operating requirements must be met, of the following, the day on which there will NOT be a sufficient number of men available to install baseball and softball backstops, a project requiring the simultaneous use of 8 men for 7 hours is

    A. Saturday   B. Monday   C. Thursday   D. Friday

19. It has become obvious that the dump truck is in need of repairs. These repairs will take two days, during which time the truck cannot be used. However, the pickup truck can be substituted for the dump truck in picking up the garbage, but requires twice the time to perform this operation.
    Of the following, the day on which the dump truck should be entered for repairs, if the operating requirements are to be met, is

    A. Monday   B. Tuesday   C. Wednesday   D. Thursday

20. Excluding the General Park Foreman and the Park Foremen, attendants, and those scheduled for a garbage pickup, the number of man-hours available for assignment on Monday is

    A. 79   B. 105   C. 114   D. 135

21. The number of man-hours expended in meeting the operating requirements during the one-week period ending June 29 is

    A. 130   B. 150   C. 200   D. 250

22. In making out the schedule for this week, the previous General Park Foreman neglected to assign enough men for Sunday, June 24, to set up benches for a concert to be given the following Monday. It is estimated that this project requires 85 man-hours and must be completed by closing hours Sunday evening.
    To complete this project and fulfill the operating requirements, the number of ADDITIONAL men for an 8-5 (8 hour) shift that must be reassigned to work on Sunday is

    A. 1   B. 2   C. 3   D. 4

23. There is a 120-acre section of grass which requires earlier than usual cutting because of its low-lying well-watered location. This section can only be cut by the Toro power mowers, which cut four acres per hour, and the hand mowers, which cut one acre per hour. Assume that one of the Toro power mowers is in the repair shop. The number of ADDITIONAL hours it will take to cut this 120-acre section of grass using the remaining grass-cutting machinery (in comparison with using all of the Toro power mowers and hand mowers) is

   A. 8   B. 10   C. 12   D. 20

24. Of those laborers and seasonal park helpers scheduled to work on Friday, the percentage that is employed in fulfilling the operating requirements is MOST NEARLY

   A. 8.2   B. 16.6   C. 23.8   D. 37.5

25. For scheduling purposes, the General Park Foreman must know how long it will take to complete the garbage collection on Monday, June 25, if both the dump truck and the pickup truck are used.
   If the pickup truck takes twice as long as the dump truck in collecting garbage, the number of hours it takes to collect the garbage using both trucks is MOST NEARLY

   A. 2.1   B. 3.2   C. 4.7   D. 6.3

# KEY (CORRECT ANSWERS)

| | | | |
|---|---|---|---|
| 1. C | | 11. C | |
| 2. B | | 12. A | |
| 3. C | | 13. D | |
| 4. A | | 14. A | |
| 5. C | | 15. A | |
| 6. A | | 16. C | |
| 7. B | | 17. C | |
| 8. C | | 18. A | |
| 9. B | | 19. B | |
| 10. C | | 20. C | |

21. B
22. D
23. A
24. B
25. C

# EXAMINATION SECTION
## TEST 1

DIRECTIONS: Each question or incomplete statement is followed by several suggested answers or completions. Select the one that BEST answers the question or completes the statement. *PRINT THE LETTER OF THE CORRECT ANSWER IN THE SPACE AT THE RIGHT.*

1. A *typical* definition of recreation agreed upon by MOST authorities would be
   A. voluntarily chosen leisure activities, for pleasure or personal benefit, meeting community standards and needs
   B. pleasurable activities provided by community agencies without social purpose
   C. whatever people want to do, because they want to do it
   D. purposeful activities, such as anti-delinquency, addiction treatment, or golden age programs, which make use of trips and cultural activities

   1.____

2. In the past, it was argued that recreation programs for youth prevented juvenile delinquency.
   Today the majority of social work or recreation authorities would MOST probably support the view that
   A. recreation is the key element in any anti-delinquency program
   B. recreation has proved to be of little value in anti-delinquency programs
   C. juvenile delinquents usually are anti-social and disruptive and should be kept out of organized recreation programs
   D. juvenile delinquency treatment requires varied services, including education, job training, recreation, and improved housing

   2.____

3. The MAJOR professional organization serving the recreation field in the United States today is the
   A. American Institute of Park and Recreation Practitioners
   B. National Recreation and Park Association
   C. National Recreation Association
   D. American Association for Health, Physical Education, and Recreation

   3.____

4. Varied theories of play have been developed by psychologists, philosophers, and others.
   One TRADITIONAL theory that sees play as the means through which children prepare for the demands of adult life is the _____ theory.
   A. instinct-practice      B. catharsis
   C. recapitulation          D. relaxation

   4.____

5. Which of the following statements BEST supports the self-expression theory of play as developed by Mason and Mitchell?
   A. Activities are engaged in for the purpose of overcoming natural human inertness.

   5.____

2 (#1)

B. Due to the pressures for self-maintenance and other compulsions, human beings use play as outlets for frustration.
C. Human physiological and anatomical structure are independent of any specific form of play.
D. Because human beings are dynamic animals, activity is a primary need of life.

6. Of the following, the MOST recent psychological theory of play is the    6.____
   A. pleasure principle theory (Freud)
   B. play extraversion theory (Piaget)
   C. arousal or stimulation theory (Berlynne)
   D. aggressive-release theory (Schiller-Spencer-Groos)

7. Generally, the BASIC philosophy of public recreation departments today is to    7.____
   A. serve all groups as fully as possible
   B. place the greatest emphasis on helping the poor
   C. serve primarily the middle and upper classes
   D. concentrate on children and youth

8. The one of the following which is NOT a widely accepted goal of public recreation departments is to    8.____
   A. provide constructive and creative outlets for leisure
   B. meet participants' physical, mental, social, and creative needs
   C. develop large numbers of athletes to play on college or pro teams
   D. strengthen family life and help community unity

9. The growth of the organized recreation movement in the United States was promoted by several social factors.    9.____
   Of the following, the one which did NOT contribute to such growth is
   A. the increase in leisure through the shortened work-week, more holidays, and longer vacations
   B. the development of movies, television, and radio as major forms of entertainment
   C. the general affluence and mobility in society
   D. more liberal attitudes toward leisure on the part of religious, educational, and government authorities

10. Recognition by state certifying boards or departments is one of the formal methods through which professionals in fields such as law or medicine are approved.    10.____
    Today, certification for recreation professionals exists in
    A. a small number of states        B. all fifty states
    C. no states                       D. about half the states

11. Supervisors should be able to advise recently appointed recreation workers on the appropriate selection of activities for specific age groups.    11.____
    When planning for after-school recreation activities for boys of elementary-school age, the MOST useful type of game would usually be

A. low-organized games, such as dodge-ball, kick-ball, and relays
B. table games, such as parcheessi, backgammon, and chess
C. encounter games and touching games, like those used in sensitivity groups
D. mental games and contests, such as ghost, coffee-pot, and twenty questions

12. Since anti-social youth are often unwilling to enter highly structured activities and programs, or may be barred from recreation centers, they are frequently not served by community recreation agencies.
Of the following, the BEST way to serve such youth is to
    A. develop entirely new kinds of activities that will appeal to delinquents because of their thrill-seeking nature
    B. organize special community center programs to serve only delinquent youth who have been in trouble with the law
    C. assign roving or street gang workers to make contact with unaffiliated youth and gangs to involve them in constructive activities
    D. wait until they are sent to correctional institutions and then give them concentrated recreation programs there

12.____

13. Adolescent girls in youth houses (detention or remand centers) often have poor self-concepts.
Of the following, the TYPICAL approach used by recreation workers in such settings to help these girls improve their self-concepts is to
    A. tell such girls at appropriate times that they are just as good as anybody
    B. organize self-improvement classes to teach skills in make-up, dressing, or modeling
    C. sponsor sports teams, such as basketball or volleyball, which can compete with other institutions
    D. administer personality tests to diagnose their problems

13.____

14. Many teenage boys are fascinated by automobiles.
Of the following, a USEFUL way for a creation worker to deal with this interest would be to
    A. sponsor drag-racing meets in a conveniently located park or raceway
    B. develop an automotive hobby car repair club in a community center or nearby garage
    C. arrange a contest to select one boy to go on a trip to the Indianapolis 500 to watch the big race
    D. develop a joint program with a school bus company to train boys as junior bus operators

14.____

15. According to the traditional *space standards* employed for the past several decades to measure the need for open space and recreation facilities in American communities, there should be AT LEAST
    A. one neighborhood playground for each 1,500 children under age 12
    B. three acres of outdoor recreation space for each 1,000 residents
    C. one acre of outdoor recreation space for each 100 residents
    D. one community center for each 5,000 children and teenagers

15.____

16. *Therapeutic recreation service* is the term applied today to programs which serve the physically, mentally, or socially handicapped.
    For BEST results, such programs should be provided in
    A. institutions such as mental hospitals or schools for the mentally handicapped
    B. community settings such as after-care centers or community programs for the physically disabled
    C. both institutional and community settings
    D. private or voluntary facilities

    16.____

17. Social group work is BEST defined as a method of social work which
    A. assigns people to groups for intensive psychotherapy as a means of crisis intervention
    B. helps people improve their social functioning and ability to cope with interpersonal problems
    C. utilizes unskilled community people to take over many social work organizations
    D. relies on the leader's ability to mobilize people into effective instruments for community reform

    17.____

18. Some recreation departments operate multi-service senior centers which provide social services related to nutrition, health needs, legal, or housing assistance, as well as recreation.
    This type of program is regarded by leading authorities in the field of recreation as
    A. usually not the function of a recreation department since it has proved to be a hindrance to customary social and recreational programs
    B. clearly not the function of a recreation department and should be discontinued
    C. an appropriate function of a recreation department and is justified by Federal funding guidelines in this field
    D. an appropriate function of a recreation department only when the program is receiving a grant from the State Department of Aging

    18.____

19. The view that MOST social workers generally have of recreation is that it is
    A. almost identical to social work
    B. a competitor with social work for public funds
    C. a medium through which they can involve and work constructively with participants
    D. strictly for fun, without a serious purpose

    19.____

20. The three MAJOR areas of social work training and practice are
    A. group work, psychiatric case work, and neighborhood management
    B. community analysis, case work, and agency supervision
    C. group rehabilitation, psychiatric community development, and case work
    D. case work, group work, and community organization

    20.____

21. Which of the following BEST expresses the program objectives of recreation programs provided by the municipal agencies as a whole?
They should
   A. emphasize after-school and summer vacation play programs
   B. provide activities for various age groups
   C. concentrate on programs for younger boys and teenage youth
   D. meet social needs that are unsatisfied by family relationships

22. Of the following, which is the LEAST appropriate basis for choosing the recreation program activities for a community center, hospital, or other institutions? The
   A. needs and interests of the participants based on their age, sex, socio-economic background, etc.
   B. overall philosophy and goals of the sponsoring agency
   C. ability of the agency to offer certain activities based on its staff resources, facilities, funding, etc.
   D. degree to which prospective participants are personally acquainted with one another

23. The MOST common approach to developing schedules of program activities in municipal recreation departments is to organize them
   A. on a centralized basis, that is, each central office or county headquarters develops a precise schedule that must be followed in each center or playground
   B. on a *report* system, that is, each center or playground develops its individual schedule and must report daily on which activities were carried out, and which were not
   C. on the basis of seasonal interests, with different schedules being developed for summer, fall, winter, and spring
   D. according to whatever seems to be of interest on a particular day, emphasizing flexibility

24. A difficult problem in scheduling recreation programs is to have personnel available at needed times.
The BEST approach for dealing with this problem is to
   A. change recreation leadership jobs to the four-day workweek that has become so popular in industry
   B. make leadership assignment schedules more flexible to insure coverage for special events, including evening and weekend activities
   C. assign all personnel a noon-to-8 P.M. daily schedule
   D. convert all full-time leadership jobs into part-time per session positions and then assign these as needed

25. Ideally, the BEST program schedule for a community recreation center would be one which covers
   A. the full day and evening to permit scheduling for senior citizens, housewives, or pre-schoolers, as well as youth and other adults
   B. from 3:00 P.M. to 10:00 P.M. since this is the time when children and youth are out of school

C. the daily hours of maximum use, based on participant demand, because of the financial limitations of many centers
D. daytime hours only since most people today will not come out at night because of fear of crime

---

## KEY (CORRECT ANSWERS)

| | | | | |
|---|---|---|---|---|
| 1. | A | | 11. | A |
| 2. | D | | 12. | C |
| 3. | B | | 13. | B |
| 4. | A | | 14. | B |
| 5. | D | | 15. | C |
| 6. | C | | 16. | C |
| 7. | A | | 17. | B |
| 8. | C | | 18. | C |
| 9. | B | | 19. | C |
| 10. | A | | 20. | D |

21. B
22. D
23. C
24. B
25. A

# TEST 2

DIRECTIONS: Each question or incomplete statement is followed by several suggested answers or completions. Select the one that BEST answers the question or completes the statement. *PRINT THE LETTER OF THE CORRECT ANSWER IN THE SPACE AT THE RIGHT.*

1. Active team games during the summer months of July and August at a neighborhood playground are BEST scheduled for
    A. early afternoon and late evening
    B. Saturday only (morning and afternoon)
    C. morning, late afternoon, and evening
    D. evening only (after 7:30 P.M.

    1._____

2. Various activities help to keep attendance at a summer playground high by building interest and enthusiasm among participants.
Which of the following is the POOREST example of such activities?
    A. Weekly special events, such as pet shows, bicycle rodeos, hobby fairs, etc.
    B. End-of-summer festivals, carnivals, play-days, exhibitions, etc., for which participants prepare for several weeks
    C. Trips using chartered or public transportation to state parks, swimming pools, etc. for those attending regularly
    D. Daily tutoring programs of remedial education for those who are having difficulty in school

    2._____

3. Of the various types of activities sponsored by public recreation departments, the MOST popular single category, according to national surveys, is
    A. services for the handicapped (such as the mentally handicapped, blind, or physical disabled)
    B. the performing arts (music, drama, and dance)
    C. social activities (clubs, parties, dances, etc.)
    D. sports of all kinds (such as baseball, football, and basketball)

    3._____

4. The MOST typical method of organizing youth sports leagues in public recreation departments is to
    A. encourage recreation leaders to organize and coach several teams themselves, running their own tournaments
    B. reduce competitive play, which is harmful to youth, and concentrate instead on cooperative games
    C. work with community organizations that set up and coach their own teams
    D. have children on each block form their own teams and do their own coaching

    4._____

5. Each craft activity has a specific set of items describing its equipment or process. The following words, *bisque, greenware,* and *slab-construction,* are used in reference to
    A. ceramics      B. metalcrafts
    C. glass-blowing   D. decoupage

    5._____

6. According to their degree of difficulty, various arts and crafts activities are usually    6.____
   suited to different age levels,
   Which of the following would be MOST suited to pre-school children?
   A. Macrame                B. Watercolor painting
   C. Fingerpainting         D  Jewelry-making

7. Among the most popular recreational sport activities are basketball, baseball,    7.____
   and bowling.
   The terms which do NOT apply to any of these three games are
   A. strike, dribble, sacrifice      B. linebacker, offside, foot-fault
   C. spare, infield, hoop            D. walking, infield, alley

8. Which of the following activities would LEAST likely be found in a municipal    8.____
   recreation department's music program?
   A. Rock-and-roll band practice and competition
   B. Chamber music groups
   C. Drum and bugle corps
   D. Informal community singing or folk music activities

9. Informal dramatics activities are often used with children and teenagers.    9.____
   Which of the following would be MOST likely to promote creative dramatic skills
   and interest among beginners?
   A. One-act play contests with scripts, costumes, and scenery
   B. Choral reading of popular poetry
   C. Memorizing and reciting sections from famous Broadway plays
   D. Improvisational dramatic games, like prop or paper bag plays

10. In the past, many recreation departments sponsored holiday festivals or    10.____
    special events such as the English May Day Festival.
    Today, the trend is to
    A. have such festivals reflect ethnic group interests such as Black Culture or
       Hispanic-American Arts
    B. eliminate all such events since there is little interest in them
    C. deal mainly with historical commemorations since these would appeal to
       traditional patriotism
    D. make festivals *future-minded* by dealing with the Space Age or America
       of the Future

11. Of the following types of tournaments, the type which can be completed MOST    11.____
    quickly in individual sports such as fencing or table-tennis is the _____
    tournament.
    A. round robin              B. elimination
    C. challenge (pyramid)      D. challenge (ladder)

12. Recreation has been affected by several key trends in psychiatric treatment.    12.____
    Which of the following is NOT such a key trend?
    A. Reducing patient populations in large, distant state institutions and setting
       up local mental health facilities, with after-care or day-clinic programs

B. Reliance on chemotherapy, which makes patients more receptive to programs
C. The development of activity therapy programs in many hospitals, which include education, recreation, occupational therapy, and similar activities
D. Hiring of psychiatric patients as recreation aides, which may lead to employment after discharge

13. In recreation programs serving the seriously physically handicapped, such as those who have suffered strokes, amputations, etc., the PRIMARY program objective is to
    A. help patients develop potential skills using the facilities of community and out-of-hospital recreational programs
    B. raise funds, through parties, bazaars, special shows, etc., that patients put on to meet special patient needs
    C. use recreation as a specific treatment modality that will restore function, help patients learn to use prosthesis, etc.
    D. make patients accept their limitations and the fact that they cannot participate in many normal recreation activities

14. The majority of mentally handicapped teenagers or young adults live in the community, rather than in institutions. Recreation for such persons has several important goals.
    Of the following, the LEAST appropriate recreation goal for such persons is to
    A. help them improve the poor coordination and overcome the obesity typical of many such persons through physical activity
    B. help them acquire social skills and improve behavior and appearance so they will be able to mingle with others more effectively
    C. provide enjoyable and socially desirable leisure activities in order to make life more satisfying
    D. improve their I.Q.'s in order to help them get better jobs or be able to continue in school

15. Senior centers that serve older persons should meet the important needs of these individuals.
    Of the following, it would be LEAST appropriate for such centers to meet the need for
    A. full-time employment by acting as a placement bureau for center members
    B. modified physical activity to help keep older people active and prevent physical deterioration
    C. social activity to help aging people make friends and avoid isolation
    D. program activities in which older people may do volunteer service in hospitals or in the community

16. In planning a recreation program at a low-income public housing project, it is important to establish an advisory board or council.
Such board or council should represent PRIMARILY the needs and interests of the
    A. civic groups
    B. residents
    C. parent-teacher associations
    D. youth workers

16.____

17. Public relations may have many objectives for a public recreation department. Of the following, the LEAST appropriate objective would be to
    A. provide accurate information about the department's overall program to the public at large
    B. encourage attendance and involvement at the department's events and regular programs
    C. build favorable public attitudes and encourage volunteer leadership in the programs
    D. encourage petitions or letter-writing campaigns for increased budgets for the department

17.____

18. The one of the following which is the MOST effective method for producing successful public relations is for recreation program administrators to
    A. appear before civil organizations
    B. satisfy users of programs
    C. publish effective brochures, announcements, and reports
    D. employ qualified, indigenous para-professionals

18.____

19. If a recreation supervisor were going to publicize a large one-day recreation event in his borough, the BEST way to promote attendance would be to
    A. use newspaper releases and distribute fliers to schools, churches, and temples
    B. place posters advertising the event in store windows
    C. put posters on playground bulletin boards
    D. make a filmstrip about the forthcoming event and distribute prints to civic groups

19.____

20. Assume that, as a recreation supervisor, you are directing a community center that has poor participation in programs by local residents.
Of the following, the MOST effective way for you to arouse more public interest would be to
    A. have the publicity office in your department's central office send out newspaper releases about the center
    B. form a neighborhood council to interpret the community's needs to you and help publicize your program
    C. frequent places where local people congregate
    D. plan a panel discussion in a nearby community auditorium to discuss the problem

20.____

5 (#2)

21. There are several possible approaches to getting community involvement in recreation service.
Of the following, the approach that would usually be LEAST workable would be to
    A. draw up a list of interested parents, clergymen, businessmen, local educators, etc., and invite them to a planning meeting about the neighborhood's recreation program
    B. announce an election to a recreation council, and select a slate of nominees, one for each square block so that local residents can elect their own representatives
    C. inquire as to whether the local Parent-Teachers Association will form a subcommittee interested in youth recreation to assist you
    D. work closely with the local district planning board to insure that they consider recreation as an important community service and to get their advice and help

21._____

22. Whether patients will be able to use their leisure constructively after discharge from the hospital is of vital concern to recreation workers in psychiatric hospitals.
Which of the following approaches would be LEAST useful in assuring continuing recreation service to a patient?
    A. Get a mimeographed list of recreation agencies in a patient's neighborhood and give him this before he is discharged
    B. Visit and talk with staff members of recreation agencies in a patient's neighborhood to make plans for their receiving the discharged patient
    C. Develop joint hospital-community recreation programs in special events, tours, entertainment programs, etc. to build a base of understanding for discharged patients
    D. Help the patient develop skills and interests in activities that will actually be available in his neighborhood after discharge

22._____

23. Therapeutic recreation seeks to help disabled persons enjoy a fuller, happier life. The question of whether they should be segregated in separate programs for the handicapped is an important one.
Which of the following statements about this group is MOST valid?
    A. The non-handicapped in society are usually very sympathetic to the disabled and welcome them in all recreational and social programs.
    B. The handicapped are better off by themselves, in groups with others having similar disabilities, so they will not feel inferior.
    C. It is an important goal to integrate the handicapped with other persons whenever possible, although sometimes it may not be feasible.
    D. The handicapped should, without exception, be mixed with the non-handicapped in recreation programs.

23._____

24. Recreation is usually considered to be a positive force for improving social relations between different racial, ethnic, or socio-economic groups.
Of the following, which is the MOST valid statement about recreation and inter-group relations?

24._____

A. Public recreation is one field in which racial discrimination is not prohibited by law.
B. Recreation workers have an obligation to reflect and agree with the views of those they serve, regardless of the nature of such views.
C. Many of our community recreation programs are heavily racially segregated.
D. Prejudice is an inborn trait which often appears in competitive sports.

25. For minority-group youth, sports often provide upward social mobility into college and subsequent business careers.
However, of the following, a MAJOR problem that arises for such youth in their seeking upward social mobility is that
   A. unscrupulous college sports programs often exploit them
   B. they are unable to satisfactorily relate to members of their peer group
   C. sports fail to provide an outlet for hostility and aggression
   D. religious cults to which they become converted distract them from sports

## KEY (CORRECT ANSWERS)

| 1. | C | | 11. | B |
|---|---|---|---|---|
| 2. | D | | 12. | D |
| 3. | D | | 13. | A |
| 4. | C | | 14. | D |
| 5. | A | | 15. | A |
| 6. | C | | 16. | B |
| 7. | B | | 17. | D |
| 8. | B | | 18. | B |
| 9. | D | | 19. | A |
| 10. | A | | 20. | B |

| 21. | B |
|---|---|
| 22. | A |
| 23. | C |
| 24. | C |
| 25. | A |

# TEST 3

DIRECTIONS: Each question or incomplete statement is followed by several suggested answers or completions. Select the one that BEST answers the question or completes the statement. *PRINT THE LETTER OF THE CORRECT ANSWER IN THE SPACE AT THE RIGHT.*

1. The trend in many recreation and park departments during the past several years has been toward providing special facilities and programs based on user fees and charges.
   The criticism MOST often made against such fees and charges is that
   A. few recreation directors have made serious efforts to serve residents of disadvantaged neighborhoods
   B. it increases the cost of servicing and maintaining facilities and services because standards must be raised
   C. public employees may be tempted to misappropriate funds or may be subject to accusations of dishonesty
   D. poor people may be unable to participate in what should be a publicly-available service

1.____

2. With few exceptions, recreation directors have not been able to gain permission to operate programs regularly in school buildings.
   Of the following, the MOST successful way to improve this situation is to
   A. develop relationships and cooperative programs with local school board and district officials, or with individual school principals and custodians
   B. bring a class-action suit against the local schoolboard
   C. collect and submit legally valid petitions to the administration
   D. exert pressure on the schools by denying them use of parks or other recreational facilities for their physical education activities

2.____

3. Many hospitals, particularly psychiatric hospitals, have therapists keep regular reports of patient participation in recreation programs.
   Of the following, the BEST use of such reports is to
   A. provide information which may be presented at meetings of the treatment team when the progress of patients is discussed
   B. provide a basis for a daily discussion between the patient and the therapist so the patient knows what is expected of him
   C. justify adverse actions such as denial of recreation privileges or the imposition of personal restrictions
   D. meet the requirements of mental hygiene laws as to standards of treatment and patient progress

3.____

4. Much correspondence is likely to come into the central office of a public recreation department.
   Generally, all letters should be answered within one or two days UNLESS
   A. a letter is of a commonplace and unimportant nature
   B. the writer is unreasonably critical of the department
   C. form letters are used in place of personalized correspondence
   D. a letter requires special inquiries or decision-making

4.____

5. One major type of report in recreation programs is based on the attendance of participants.
   Such report are GENERALLY considered to be
   A. an excellent quantitative and qualitative basis for evaluating the success of a program
   B. of primary use in operational research involving participant behavior and outcomes
   C. unnecessary since few departments continue to use attendance reports as a basis for funding
   D. quite inaccurate unless attendance counts are done systematically and staff members avoid inflating them

5._____

6. An informal survey of recreation in a hospital showed that patients who engaged regularly in the program were discharged from the hospital earlier than those who did not.
   Based on this information only, it would be MOST valid to say that
   A. such information has validity or meaning only to a qualified medical research person
   B. it is inconclusive whether there exists a cause and effect relationship between participation and discharge
   C. probably the healthier patients took part in the recreation program, and this was the reason for their earlier discharge
   D. recreation was the major determinant of earlier discharge

6._____

7. The one of the following it would be BEST to do when preparing or developing an annual report of a large recreational program is to
   A. gather material such as photos, program descriptions, news stories, and statistics which appeared during the courses of the year
   B. use narrative description rather than charts or graphs to present statistical data
   C. present only the positive aspects and successes of your program, elaborating when necessary to give a favorable picture
   D. give praise to key political figures in the report so they will support the program in the future

7._____

8. *Crash* programs of recreation have sometimes been rushed into slum areas as a response to the threat of violence. Often, the approach has been to present *portable* programs, for example, portable pools put into lots of streets, mobile libraries and nature displays, puppet shows, movies, and rock or soul music shows.
   Of the following, the MAJOR weakness of the *portable* recreation approach is that
   A. funds expended for such programs tend to be excessive and the general public is antagonized
   B. it emphasizes expending aimless energy rather than promoting social growth
   C. it meets only temporary recreation needs and fails to effect a permanent resolution of recreation problems

8._____

D. it tends to draw large numbers of youth out on the street, where they become riotous

9. A recent change in the concept of recreation as a public service is that it is now being thought of as a kind of social therapy.
The MOST recent illustration of this has been the
   A. joint effort of religious agencies to develop new recreation programs, including year-round camping, for broken families
   B. expanded recreation programs in youth houses, remand institutions, and similar institutions run by the Department of Social Services
   C. new recreation program in private or multi-room occupancy hotels
   D. crash effort to provide recreation programs for alcoholics and older drug addicts

9.____

10. Low-income and racial minority youth tend to have very limited recreation interests. Often, teenage boys want to take part in basketball, but little else of an organized nature.
For a recreation center director, what would be the BEST professional approach to this attitude?
   A. Begin with the interests they already have, then try to broaden their involvement in other recreation, athletic, or cultural activities
   B. Stick to basketball, their true interest, since they resist other activities
   C. Since they are able to play basketball in many neighborhood settings, eliminate this part of the program and offer new kinds of sports, cultural activities, and social events
   D. Rely on carefully prepared interest survey, and then offer youth only the activities and events they say they want

10.____

11. A NEW trend in many cities, with respect to the assignment of recreation leadership personnel, is to
   A. assign workers to one setting on a full-time, year-round basis so that they will be completely familiar with the work and do a superior job
   B. use seniority more than ever before, thereby giving the long-time employee freedom to pick his job
   C. rotate the assignments of workers from season-to-season or even day-to-day maximize output and improve morale by giving challenging assignments
   D. create new job shifts, such as one week from 9:00 to 5:00, next week from 2:00 to 10:00, etc.

11.____

12. Recreation counseling is becoming more widely used in many hospitals. Such counseling is PRIMARILY intended to
   A. help patients explore their leisure attitudes and interests and motivate them toward fuller participation after discharge
   B. teach patients a broad range of activities, such as sports, crafts, and social skills, that they can use after discharge
   C. use the recreation situation to uncover problems that can then be discussed when the patient gets therapeutic counseling

12.____

D. allow the patients to advise staff members on how best to organize the recreation program

13. A major problem today in many recreation and park departments is costly and destructive vandalism.
Which of the following methods of dealing with this problem has NOT been widely accepted throughout the United States?
    A. Provide stronger enforcement of rules and better surveillance and protection of recreation and park facilities
    B. Offer more attractive programs since people are less likely to vandalize a facility if it is staffed and providing popular community activities
    C. Use new types of designs so that facilities are less prone to vandalism, such as windowless buildings, concrete benches and tables, etc.
    D. Abandon parks or playgrounds that have been repeatedly vandalized

13._____

14. The Board of Education has a strong commitment to recreation.
Its recreation program focuses CHIEFLY on
    A. adult education programs in adult centers
    B. children and youth in after-school and evening centers
    C. the categories of pre-school, mentally handicapped, and senior citizens
    D. youth either considered to be pre-delinquent or adjudicated as delinquent

14._____

15. Those working to provide recreation to persons who have a physical, mental, emotional, or social disability frequently seek assistance from social service agencies.
Which of the following pairs of agencies is LEAST likely to be helpful to them?
    A. Catholic Charities; Federation of Protestant Welfare Agencies
    B. United Cerebral Palsy of N.Y.C.; New York Association for the Blind
    C. New York Association for Retarded Children; National Wheelchair Athletic Association
    D. New York League for Crippled and Disabled Children, Adults and Aging; Handclasp for the Handicapped, Inc.

15._____

16. Throughout the nation, there has been an increase in senior centers for aging persons.
Which of the following agencies does NOT sponsor special centers for aging persons?
    A. Housing Authority's low-income projects
    B. Office of Continuing Education
    C. Parks, Recreation and Cultural Affairs Administration
    D. Department of Social Services

16._____

17. The municipal department that has the PRIMARY responsibility for providing social services for youth, including recreation, is the
    A. Youth Activities Board
    B. Youth Services Agency
    C. United Block Association for Youth
    D. Bureau of Youth Community Services

17._____

18. If a recreation center director had severe problems with drug users in his neighborhood, the APPROPRIATE municipal department for him to ask for assistance is the    18.____
    A. Health and Hospitals Corporation
    B. Syanon or Phoenix House
    C. Department of Correction
    D. Addiction Services Agency

Questions 19-20.

DIRECTIONS: Questions 19 and 20 are to be answered SOLELY on the basis of the following passage.

This country was built on the puritanical belief that honest toil was the foundation of moral rectitude, the cement of society, and the uphill road to progress. Idleness was sin. As a result, we treat free time today as a conditional joy. We permit ourselves to relax only as a reward for hard work or as the recreation needed to put us back into shape for the job. Thus, the aimless delightful play of children gives way in adult life to a serious dedication to golf, the game that is so good for business.

19. According to the above passage, during former times in this country, respectable    19.____
    work was considered to be MOST NEARLY a
    A. way to improve health         B. form of recreation
    C. developer of good character   D. reward for leisure

20. According to the point of view presented in the above passage, it would be    20.____
    MOST reasonable to assume that an employer would consider an employee's vacation to be a time for the employee to
    A. determine his own leisure time priorities
    B. loaf and relax
    C. learn new recreational skills
    D. increase his effectiveness at work

Questions 21-23.

DIRECTIONS: Questions 21 through 23 are to be answered SOLELY on the basis of the following passage.

One of the key supervisory problems in a large municipal recreation department is that many leaders are assigned to isolated playgrounds or small centers, where it is difficult to observe their work regularly. Often their facilities are extremely limited. In such settings, as well as in larger recreation centers, where many recreation leaders tend to have other jobs as well, there tends to be a low level of morale and incentive. Still, it is the supervisor's task to help recreation personnel to develop pride in their work, and to maintain a high level of performance. With isolated leaders, the supervisor may give advice or assistance. Leaders may be assigned to different tasks or settings during the year to maximize their productivity and provide new challenges. When it is clear that leaders are not willing to make a real effort to contribute to the department, the possibility of penalties must be considered, within the scope of departmental policy and the union contract. However, the supervisor should be constructive, encourage and assist workers to take a greater interest in their work, be innovative, and try to raise morale and to improve performance in positive ways.

21. The one of the following that would be the MOST appropriate title for the foregoing passage is 21.____
    A. SMALL COMMUNITY CENTERS – PRO AND CON
    B. PLANNING BETTER RECREATION PROGRAMS
    C. THE SUPERVISOR'S TASK IN UPGRADING PERSONNEL PERFORMANCE
    D. THE SUPERVISOR AND THE MUNICIPAL UNION – RIGHTS AND OBLIGATIONS

22. The above passage makes clear that recreation leadership performance in ALL recreation playgrounds and centers throughout a large city is 22.____
    A. generally above average, with good morale on the part of most recreation leaders
    B. beyond description since no one has ever observed or evaluated leaders
    C. a key test of the personnel department's effort to develop more effective hiring standards
    D. of mixed quality, with many recreation leaders having poor morale and a low level of achievement

23. According to the above passage, the supervisor's role is to 23.____
    A. use disciplinary action as his major tool in upgrading performance
    B. tolerate the lack of effort of individual employees since they are assigned to isolated playgrounds or small centers
    C. employ encouragement, advice, and, when appropriate, disciplinary action to improve performance
    D. inform the county supervisor whenever malfeasance or idleness is detected

Questions 24-25.

DIRECTIONS: Questions 24 and 25 are to be answered SOLELY on the basis of the following passage.

A recent study revealed some very concrete evidence concerning the relationship between avocations and mental health. A number of well-adjusted persons were surveyed as to the type, number, and duration of their hobbies. The findings were compared to those from a similar survey of mentally disturbed persons. In the well-adjusted group, both the number of hobbies and the intensity with which they were pursued were far greater than that of the mentally disturbed group.

24. According to the above passage, the study showed that 24.____
    A. well-adjusted people engage in hobbies more widely and deeply than do mentally disturbed people
    B. hobbies, if taken seriously, serve to keep most people mentally well

C. mental patients should be taught hobbies as a part of their therapy
D. the degree of interest in hobbies plays an important role in maintaining good mental health

25. In reference to the study mentioned in the above passage, it is MOST accurate to say that it appears to have     25.____
    A. been based on a carefully-structured, complex research design
    B. considered the variables of mental health and hobby involvement
    C. contained a general definition of mental health
    D. given evidence of a causal relationship between hobbies and mental health

---

## KEY (CORRECT ANSWERS)

| | | | |
|---|---|---|---|
| 1. | D | 11. | C |
| 2. | A | 12. | A |
| 3. | A | 13. | D |
| 4. | D | 14. | B |
| 5. | D | 15. | D |
| 6. | B | 16. | B |
| 7. | A | 17. | B |
| 8. | C | 18. | D |
| 9. | B | 19. | C |
| 10. | A | 20. | D |

21. C
22. D
23. C
24. A
25. B

# EXAMINATION SECTION
## TEST 1

DIRECTIONS: Each question or incomplete statement is followed by several suggested answers or completions. Select the one that BEST answers the question or completes the statement. *PRINT THE LETTER OF THE CORRECT ANSWER IN THE SPACE AT THE RIGHT.*

1. A type of depression or pit that may serve to drain, collect or store liquids is called a  1.____
   A. ditch   B. gutter   C. sump   D. trench

2. The general name applied to the material that is spread on the ground around plants to prevent evaporation of water from the soil or the freezing of the roots is  2.____
   A. mulch   B. mullock   C. fertilizer   D. mullion

3. The wire, rope, chain or rod that is attached to a tree, and which is used to steady the tree, is called a  3.____
   A. guy   B. davit   C. hoist   D. bitt

4. A chemical used to kill weeds is called a  4.____
   A. pesticide   B. herbicide   C. fungicide   D. arborcide

5. A mixture of cement or lime with sand and water which is used between bricks or stones in buildings is called  5.____
   A. epoxy   B. putty   C. concrete   D. mortar

6. Coarse aggregate is the same as  6.____
   A. pumice   B. cement
   C. crushed stone   D. sand

7. The process of keeping the surface of concrete as wet as possible after the concrete is placed and hardened in order to prevent loss of water through evaporation is called  7.____
   A. floating   B. damping   C. curing   D. checking

8. Plants that live for more than two years are called  8.____
   A. annuals   B. perennials   C. biennials   D. semi-annuals

9. Which piece of equipment is run by compressed air?  9.____
   A. Drill press   B. Impact wrench
   C. Soldering gun   D. Jack hammer

QUESTIONS 10-13.

Answer questions 10-13 SOLELY on the basis of the information given in the paragraphs below.

NITROGEN AND PLANT GROWTH

Nitrogen is an essential element for plant growth. Its most important function is to stimulate vegatative development and it is, therefore, particularly necessary in the production of leaves and stems. If an excess of nitrogen is applied to the soil, it will result in an excessive growth of foliage at the expense of flowers and fruit. The cell walls of the stems will also become weakened and the plant's resistance to disease will be lowered.

Nitrogen is seldom found in the soil in a free state but is usually in combination with other elements. Soils are usually lowest in available nitrogen during the early spring months. It is at this season that quickly available nitrogenous fertilizers are of particular value.

10. According to the paragraph, an excess of nitrogen in plants is *likely to* produce

    A. strong healthy stems
    B. stronger resistance to disease
    C. too many leaves and stems
    D. too many flowers and fruit.

11. Weakened cell walls and decreased resistance to disease in plants are *likely to* occur because

    A. there is too much foliage on the plant
    B. there is not enough nitrogen in the soil
    C. there is too much nitrogen in the soil
    D. there are too many flowers or too much fruit on the plant

12. According to the above passage, one of the properties of nitrogen is that it

    A. seldom combines with other elements in the soil
    B. increase the production of flowers
    C. increases the growth of roots
    D. increases vegetative growth in a plant

13. In which months would soil *most likely* be LOWEST in nitrogen? Late

    A. March and early April
    B. June and early July
    C. September and early October
    D. December and early January

14. A person may appear to be accident-prone for a number of reasons. Which of the following would NOT usually be particularly associated with frequent accidents?

    A. Slow work habits
    B. Improper training
    C. Lack of physical coordination
    D. Working in cramped quarters

15. When removing a large branch from a tree, a pruner usually includes an undercut on the branch.
    The SPECIFIC purpose of the undercut is to

    A. stimulate the flow of sap to the area where the branch is taken off in order to stimulate growth of new branches
    B. prevent the branch that is being taken off from tearing off a strip of bark down the tree
    C. aid the wound from the cut off branch to heal quickly without decay or infection
    D. prevent an excessive growth of new branches from where the branch had been

16. A foreman sees one of his men start to cut a hedge so that it will be narrower at the bottom than at the top. The foreman stops the man and tells him to cut hedges in general so that they are narrower at the top than at the bottom. "Why?" asks the man.
    The foreman gave him the *generally accepted* reason, which is that

    A. rainfall will be able to run down the sides, and moisture will reach other parts of the hedge more quickly
    B. the broad base of the hedge will keep the hedge from being top-heavy and prevent it from toppling over during heavy winds
    C. sunlight will be able to reach all parts of the hedge, thereby helping to keep the growth of the entire hedge dense
    D. the hedge will be uniform from top to bottom since the top grows out much faster than the bottom

17. Concrete sidewalks are usually laid with a divider space every four or six feet rather than as one long ribbon.
    The reason for allowing the space is that in the summer the concrete in the sidewalk is *most likely* to

    A. contract    B. expand    C. sweat    D. soften

18. Some degree of shock accompanies all injuries. Symptoms of shock include all of the following EXCEPT

    A. a warm dry skin           B. a rapid, weak pulse
    C. enlarged pupils           D. irregular breathing

19. You are going to plant ivy in the circular flower bed pictured in Figure I. You have decided to plant them on the border of each of circles A, B, and C. The distance around each of the circles is as follows:
    A = 32 feet
    B = 20 feet
    C = 6 feet
    If you can plant 3 plants per foot, how many plants will you need?

    A. 100    B. 135    C. 156    D. 174

20. Nine out of ten people have never used a fire extinguisher. A trained person used a fire extinguisher 2 1/2 times more effectively than the average person does.
    These facts should motivate a foreman of a new crew exposed to possible fire hazards to

A. have a substitute for fire extinguishers on the job
B. rely only on experienced firemen for extinguishing fires
C. try to get men into his crew who are experienced in the use of fire extinguishers
D. give training to his men on the use of fire extinguishers

21. The crowbar, pick and shovel are three hand tools that can all be used *effectively* and *safely* in the process of

    A. splitting logs
    B. prying heavy objects
    C. making holes in stone
    D. digging up earth

22. Those tools which require the user to twist or turn one end in one direction while the other end is held fast in order to apply a force on an object are classified as torsion tools. Of the following, the one which would NOT be classified as a torsion tool is

    A. pliers    B. wrench    C. pinchbar    D. screw driver

23. A portable heater used widely in severe weather to protect masonry, concrete and plaster from freezing and to provide warmth for workmen is the

    A. blowtorch
    B. salamander
    C. plumbers' furnace
    D. metal forge

24. In loading and unloading materials a variety of equipment is used.
Of the following, the one which is generally NOT an accessory in moving materials onto and off trucks is a

    A. power shovel
    B. clam shell
    C. grease rack
    D. lift truck

25. Which one of the following pictures shows the top of a Phillips-type screw?

26. Which one of the following is called a box-end wrench?

27. A chisel is a hammer-struck tool. Some workmen grip the chisel with the fist to steady it and minimize the chances of glancing blows. The turn "glancing" refers here to the

    A. hammer striking the chisel off angle, thereby hitting the hand holding the chisel
    B. chisel bending or warping under the pressure of hammer blows
    C. hammer hitting with uneven force each time it contacts the chisel
    D. chisel striking the material to be cut straight on, instead of at an angle

28. Which one of the following BEST describes a *counters ink*? A

    A. tool designed to balance weight
    B. hammer used to shape sheet metal
    C. tool that enlarges the top part of a hole
    D. tool used to dig holes rapidly

29. Of the following, the MAIN reason that some electrical tools require the use of a 3-pronged plug is to

    A. prolong the life of the fuse
    B. avoid wasting electricity
    C. prolong the life of the cord
    D. properly ground them

30. Which of the following statements applies BEST to the care and use of a shovel?

    A. A shovel should not be waxed or greased immediately before using it.
    B. Dipping a shovel into a pail of water occasionally, while digging, makes the shovel easier to use.
    C. The leg muscles should not be permitted to take most of the load when shovelling.
    D. A shovel should lie flat on the ground when it is not being used.

31. Which is the SAFEST distance between the base of a 24-foot fully extended ladder and the base of the building against which it is placed?

    A. 3 feet    B. 6 feet    C. 9 feet    D. 12 feet

32. When instructing a man on how to lift a heavy object, you should advise him to

    A. stand as far from the load as possible
    B. keep the back as straight as possible
    C. lift by straightening his legs first and then his back
    D. lift from a full crouch

33. Suppose that, of 14 men assigned to a shop, 3 are absent. The percentage of men absent is, *most nearly*,

    A. 19%    B. 20%    C. 21%    D. 22%

34. The sum of 5 1/6 + 7 1/3 + 4 1/2 + 3 1/8 is

    A. 19 7/8    B. 20 1/2    C. 20 3/4    D. 20 7/8

35. A foreman must order enough sod to cover a dirt area 36 feet wide by 28 feet long. Each piece of sod is 3 feet long by 12 inches wide.
How many pieces of sod should be ordered to cover that area?

   A. 192   B. 236   C. 304   D. 336

36. If each man works at the same speed and 6 men take 2 1/2 hours to do a particular job, how many men will it take to do the *same* job in 1 hour?

   A. 13   B. 15   C. 26   D. 30

37. An agency bought 115 hammers from Company A for $253.00. It later bought 80 hammers from Company B for $140.00 If the agency had bought all of its hammers from Company B, the TOTAL AMOUNT of money that would have been *saved* would have been

   A. $25.25   B. $45.00   C. $51.75   D. $63.25

38. In order to make up a particular mixture of concrete, a foreman mixes 2 parts of cement to 3 parts of sand and 4 parts of gravel.
If he wants to make up 405 lbs. of concrete, he would need

   A. 45 lbs. of cement, 170 lbs. of sand, and 190 lbs. of gravel
   B. 45 lbs. of cement, 160 lbs. of sand, and 200 lbs. of gravel
   C. 90 lbs. of cement, 140 lbs. of sand, and 175 lbs. of gravel
   D. 90 lbs. of cement, 135 lbs. of sand, and 180 lbs. of gravel

39. A tank that is 5/8 full is holding 200 gallons of gasoline. The amount of gasoline this tank can hold *when filled* to capacity is

   A. 270 gals.   B. 320 gals.   C. 360 gals.   D. 410 gals.

40.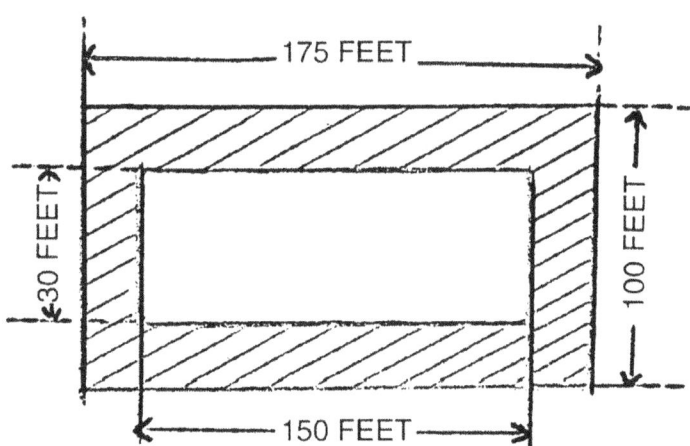

The shaded portion of the above drawing represents an icy walk surrounding a building. If it takes 1 lb. of rock salt to clear ice from every 100 square feet of walk, how many pounds of rock salt would be needed to clear the *entire* walk?

   A. 55   B. 60   C. 120   D. 175

## KEY (CORRECT ANSWERS)

| | | | |
|---|---|---|---|
| 1. C | 11. C | 21. D | 31. B |
| 2. A | 12. D | 22. C | 32. B |
| 3. A | 13. A | 23. B | 33. C |
| 4. B | 14. A | 24. C | 34. A |
| 5. D | 15. B | 25. B | 35. D |
| 6. C | 16. C | 26. C | 36. B |
| 7. C | 17. B | 27. A | 37. C |
| 8. B | 18. A | 28. C | 38. D |
| 9. D | 19. D | 29. D | 39. B |
| 10. C | 20. D | 30. B | 40. A |

# EXAMINATION SECTION
## TEST 1

DIRECTIONS: Each question or incomplete statement is followed by several suggested answers or completions. Select the one that BEST answers the question or completes the statement. *PRINT THE LETTER OF THE CORRECT ANSWER IN THE SPACE AT THE RIGHT.*

1. Which of the following is the BEST measure to take to discipline a worker for his first violation of a rule?

    A. Speak to him in private
    B. Point out his past mistakes
    C. Explain to him the grievance procedure
    D. Have some witnesses present

2. When a supervisor gives verbal instructions to a maintainer about the procedure to follow in doing a certain job, the supervisor will MOST likely avoid confusing the maintainer if

    A. his instructions are clear and concise
    B. his instructions contain as many details as possible
    C. he gives the instructions to the maintainer as quickly as possible
    D. he repeats the instructions to the maintainer several times, each time using different words

3. Of the following, the BEST procedure to follow if you see one of your men using the wrong tool in doing his work is to

    A. stop him from proceeding and let another maintainer finish this man's work
    B. stop him from proceeding and direct him to use the correct tool
    C. take the man aside after the job is finished and tell him not to use the wrong tool again
    D. reprimand him and avoid giving him this type of work in the future

4. Of the following, the LEAST appropriate guide for a supervisor to follow in assigning his men to various jobs is for him to

    A. assign the work according to each man's ability
    B. allow his men to take on as many jobs as they think they can handle
    C. distribute the workload evenly
    D. combine similar jobs and assign them to the same men

5. The term *shoestring parks* MOST correctly describes

    A. foot paths, bicycle paths, and passive recreational areas developed alongside the pavements of parkways
    B. recreational areas developed along the beach areas under the jurisdiction of the department of parks
    C. playgrounds and small parks developed on excess lands purchased for public housing projects
    D. play areas developed in conjunction with large public swimming pools

6. A maintainer asks his supervisor a question about a new maintenance procedure with which the supervisor is not familiar.
Of the following actions, the BEST one for the supervisor to take is to tell the maintainer

   A. to try to logically figure out the new procedure
   B. to use the old method with which the maintainer is more familiar
   C. that he should try to find another supervisor who knows the answer
   D. that he will try to get the information for him

7. Of the following, the MOST important reason for having the employee suggestion program is that it

   A. makes employees realize that management's job is not an easy one
   B. is a suitable replacement for the *merit increase*
   C. saves the department money
   D. gives employees an alternate route for their grievance

8. The MOST important function of fences around playgrounds is that

   A. fences eliminate vandalism by keeping out the mischief makers and putting the playgrounds under complete control
   B. adequate fencing relieves the department of all liability in cases of injury occurring at times when the playground is locked
   C. children using a playground are less likely to be injured in auto accidents on streets adjacent to the playground if it is fenced
   D. fences add to the value of adjacent property by reducing trespassing by children using the playground

9. It has been suggested that where a playground borders on a busy street, the entrances should be at the corners rather than in the middle of the block. The MOST important basis for this suggestion is

   A. fencing costs will be reduced considerably by such construction
   B. children leaving the playground will not be able to run into the street between intersections
   C. clearing the playground of children will be accomplished more easily and in a more orderly fashion
   D. roads and paths will be reduced to the desired minimum

10. Chainlink fences are generally considered the MOST satisfactory fencing for playgrounds and athletic fields because

    A. their maintenance requirements are less than for iron picket fences
    B. they economize on space in playgrounds
    C. they enable the playground to be locked when not in use
    D. they fit into a landscaping design more satisfactorily than any other type of fence

11. The dimension of a standard city block is 800 feet by 200 feet. The acreage of this block is MOST NEARLY _____ acres.

    A. 4    B. 2 1/2    C. 8    D. 1 1/2

12. Of the following instructions concerning the reporting of an accident, the one which is LEAST correct is

    A. park conditions contributing to the cause of the accident should be noted
    B. note all damage to park property
    C. ascertain the name of the owner and license number if an auto was involved
    D. report on the condition of the brakes if an auto is involved

13. The park use for which a park permit is NOT required is

    A. an organized picnic or outing
    B. fishing in designated areas
    C. storage of boats on park lands
    D. private construction work not under contract with the commissioner

14. Assume that you are a supervisor and that a maintainer makes a complaint to you which has no merit.
    Of the following, the BEST way for you to handle this situation is to

    A. tell the maintainer not to bother you with worthless complaints
    B. keep the complaint on file and ignore it as long as possible
    C. forward the complaint to your assistant supervisor
    D. discuss the complaint with him and show him that his complaint is not justified

15. As a newly appointed supervisor, you find that one of your workers is a longtime friend whom you must now supervise.
    Of the following, your BEST course of action is to

    A. break off all relations with this employee
    B. attempt to separate your official actions from your personal attitudes
    C. do nothing unless the other men complain of favoritism on your part
    D. request that your friend be transferred to another supervisor

16. Of the following, the dual use of play space is MOST feasible in the case of a

    A. tennis court used for volleyball
    B. paddle tennis court used for regulation tennis
    C. golf course used for regulation baseball
    D. shuffleboard course used for paddle tennis

17. Of the following, a tree that is LEAST preferred for street planting is the

    A. pin oak              B. red maple
    C. plane                D. silver maple

18. The maintenance of newly planted street trees is the responsibility of the

    A. homeowner for the first year, and thereafter the department of parks
    B. department of parks as soon as the planting of the tree is completed
    C. both the home owner and the department of parks as soon as they are planted
    D. department of parks only if the home owner duly notifies the department that he wishes to relieve himself of responsibility

19. To maintain corn brooms and fibre brushes in good condition, the park supervisor should instruct his employees to

    A. avoid wetting them with water since they may become brittle if so treated
    B. treat the fibres with oil regularly to keep them flexible
    C. discard those brooms which have become worn down or are brittle
    D. wet them once or twice a week with warm water to prevent them from becoming brittle

20. During the summer season, the supervisor should maintain a cleaning schedule in which the floors of comfort station toilet rooms are swept

    A. and wet mopped daily
    B. and damp mopped daily and washed once a week
    C. daily and damp mopped weekly
    D. daily and mopped every other day

21. Of the following, the MOST important reason for NOT using deodorants in cleaning comfort station floors is deodorants

    A. may cover up the odor, but not eliminate the source
    B. have an unpleasant odor which requires excessive ventilation of the rooms
    C. may contain chemicals that will harm the surfaces cleaned
    D. reduce the effectiveness of cleaning solutions used on these floors

22. If the car which you are driving starts to skid on a wet pavement, the BEST way to overcome the skidding is to

    A. put on the emergency brake in addition to the foot brake
    B. release the brake and turn the steering wheel opposite to the direction in which the car is skidding
    C. release the brake and turn the steering wheel in the direction in which the car is skidding
    D. disengage the clutch and brake and try to keep the wheels straight ahead

23. Concerning the use of oil in crankcases of automobiles, it is CORRECT to say that

    A. lighter oils should be used in the wintertime
    B. lighter oils should be used in the summertime
    C. heavy oils should be used in the wintertime
    D. oil should not be changed if the oil gage shows full

24. The preferred method of eliminating growths of algae in a wading pool or swimming pool is to

    A. dose the water with copper sulphate
    B. increase the concentration of chlorine dosage
    C. empty the pool immediately upon discovering these growths
    D. spray the water surface with a 10% solution of D.D.T.

25. The routine of swimming pool operation includes

    A. tests of chlorine content of the water once a day
    B. cleaning filter beds with raw water rather than filtered water
    C. recirculation of water used in backwashing filter beds
    D. use of alum in the filter plants of the pool to form a floc

26. When the water in a wading pool appears excessively dirty, the MOST appropriate action the supervisor should take is to

   A. increase the rate of flow of water into the pool and clean the drains
   B. have the pool drained, cleaned, and refilled
   C. dose the pool more heavily with chlorine solution to reduce the possibility of infection spread
   D. forbid children to enter the pool unless they are clean

27. In preparing and maintaining a large wading pool for winter use as an ice skating rink, the supervisor should be careful to

   A. keep drainage outlets open to take up excess water
   B. build up the surface by applying water in thin film-like layers
   C. flood the area each morning to maintain the ice surface prepared previously
   D. apply water first to the area nearest the water sup-ply outlet and then proceed towards the far end

28. In maintaining clay tennis courts, the park foreman should have his employee apply calcium chloride to the surface primarily in order to

   A. reduce acidity of the surface
   B. keep dust down
   C. increase surface drainage
   D. keep the surface even

29. The material that is NOT used in marking the foul lines on a baseball field with a grass surface is

   A. white lead           B. lime
   C. cold water calcimine D. whiting

30. Of the following, the statement that is CORRECT with respect to the maintenance of playground equipment is

   A. bearings of seesaws and swings should be greased daily to prevent excessive wear
   B. galvanized steel piping of jungle gyms should be oiled periodically during the summer to reduce rusting and deterioration
   C. bolts and nuts used on equipment should be checked daily for tightness and wear
   D. chutes of slides require daily waxing to preserve a smooth surface

31. The newer type of sandpits have irrigation systems for cleaning the sand. The advantage of these pits is that

   A. they require less maintenance than the older type
   B. they are less costly to install
   C. the sand surface need not be raked to remove debris
   D. the sand need not be replaced as frequently as in the older type

32. The manufacturer's name with which some lawnmowers in the department of parks are associated is

   A. Toro    B. Royer    C. Hardie    D. Kaiser

33. CORRECT practice with respect to the sprinkling of lawns includes the fact that 33.___
    A. regular sprinkling of lawns should begin in the early spring when the ground thaws
    B. sprinkling should always be continued on any one spot until the soil has become thoroughly drenched with water
    C. sprinkling should never be begun in the late afternoon or early evening
    D. whirling spray-type sprinklers should not be used unless the soil is excessively dry and powdery

34. Generally, it is better to seed a lawn in the fall than in the spring. Of the following, the BEST explanation for this gardening rule is 34.___
    A. the ground is dryer in the spring than in the fall
    B. tree shading is at a minimum in the fall
    C. pedestrian traffic over a lawn is at a minimum in the fall
    D. weed growth is less in the fall than in the spring

35. In mowing a lawn, the blades of the mower should usually be adjusted to maintain the height of the grass 35.___
    A. about one-half inch
    B. not less than one and one-half inches
    C. not less than three inches
    D. approximately one inch

36. In giving instructions to laborers assigned to mowing a lawn, it should be emphasized that 36.___
    A. mowing should be frequent in hot dry weather since grass grows rapidly during this period
    B. clippings should generally be removed after mowing when lawns are regularly mowed
    C. lawnmowers should be operated up to the trunks of surrounding trees to insure an even turf
    D. lawns should not be mowed when wet and soft to avoid injury to the turf

37. In the maintenance and operation of lawnmowers, the park groundskeeper should be sure that 37.___
    A. lawns are sprayed with water just before mowing
    B. the revolving blades are pressed close to the stationary or non-revolving blade, with no clearance, if possible
    C. lawns are raked clean before mowing is attempted
    D. lawns are raked clean after regular mowing

38. To overcome brown spots on a lawn, the groundskeeper should have the lawn treated with 38.___
    A. D.D.T.                          B. lead arsenate
    C. mercury compounds               D. heavy water spray

39. 2,4-D is a chemical which the groundskeeper should use to

    A. control weed growth on lawns
    B. destroy Japanese beetle grubs in the soil
    C. control grass diseases
    D. destroy bark beetles

40. An ingredient that is NOT usually found in compost is

    A. lime
    C. manure
    B. calcium chloride
    D. leaves

---

## KEY (CORRECT ANSWERS)

| | | | |
|---|---|---|---|
| 1. A | 11. A | 21. A | 31. D |
| 2. A | 12. D | 22. C | 32. A |
| 3. B | 13. B | 23. A | 33. B |
| 4. B | 14. D | 24. A | 34. D |
| 5. A | 15. B | 25. D | 35. B |
| 6. D | 16. A | 26. B | 36. D |
| 7. C | 17. D | 27. B | 37. C |
| 8. C | 18. A | 28. B | 38. C |
| 9. B | 19. D | 29. A | 39. A |
| 10. A | 20. A | 30. C | 40. B |

# TEST 2

DIRECTIONS: Each question or incomplete statement is followed by several suggested answers or completions. Select the one that BEST answers the question or completes the statement. *PRINT THE LETTER OF THE CORRECT ANSWER IN THE SPACE AT THE RIGHT.*

1. In gathering leaves and twigs, the large wooden rake should be used with

   A. long sliding strokes, the prongs being lifted only to clear the debris
   B. short pull and push strokes to avoid tearing the sod
   C. brush strokes as with a broom
   D. long pushing strokes, forcing leaves and twigs away from you

2. The newer type of fountains installed in parks and playgrounds throws the water jet at an angle instead of vertically. It is thought that the newer type is superior because

   A. the desired height of the jet of water is obtained more easily
   B. such fountains are more attractive and fit in better with modern playground layouts
   C. the possibility of damage and vandalism is reduced
   D. the possibility of contamination of the water supply is reduced

3. Of the following, the MOST important reason for shutting off the water supply to drinking fountains in the late fall is

   A. there is less need for water in the late fall and winter
   B. to avoid vandalism due to reduction of forces after the summer season
   C. to avoid breakage of supply lines in the winter
   D. water supply lines to fountains are usually located below the frost line

4. Suppose that a laborer complains to you about flooding of low parts of walks and paths in his park after heavy rains.
   Of the following, the factor that you would NOT consider as a probable cause of flooding is the

   A. condition of catch basins in the park
   B. condition of the street sewer system adjacent to the park
   C. condition of drainage system of the comfort stations in the park
   D. clogging of drainage lines and inlets

5. The repainting of iron picket fences should preferably be scheduled for

   A. any time in the fall or early winter, depending only on the number of visitors to the park involved
   B. early mornings in the late summer or fall months because the temperature is low
   C. winter weather, since cold weather is an aid to quick drying of paint
   D. early afternoons of clear dry days in the late summer or early fall

6. A priming coat of red lead is usually painted on iron picket fences MAINLY because

   A. the color of the finish coat will show up better on red lead
   B. it cleans the metal surface of rust and other foreign particles
   C. it prevents rusting and corrosion of the iron fence
   D. it avoids blistering of the finish paint coat

7. A laborer has been assigned to a playground containing a comfort station which is heated by a low pressure oil burner in the wintertime. Your instructions to the laborer regarding the operation of the heating plant should include

   A. maintenance of steam pressure above 10 pounds
   B. daily cleaning of ignition electrodes
   C. daily replacement of boiler water to prevent rust formation
   D. inspection of water level daily before starting up

   7.____

8. A wire brush is USUALLY used in

   A. removing rust stains from the porcelain surface of wash basins
   B. preparing iron surfaces for painting
   C. heavy sweeping of concrete and cement surfaces
   D. clearing roofs of comfort stations of accumulated rubbish

   8.____

9. The tool which is LEAST likely to be used by a worker in the replacement and repair of wood slats of benches is

   A. hack saw        B. plane
   C. cross-cut saw   D. brace and bit

   9.____

10. Seesaws should be inspected daily to

    A. determine the need for painting the wood parts
    B. check possible splintering of the seat ends
    C. avoid rusting of metal supports
    D. see that horizontal pipe supports are not more than 24 inches above the ground

    10.____

11. For sharpening gardening and pruning shears, the tool used is a(n)

    A. whetstone      B. oil stone
    C. flat file      D. carborundum wheel

    11.____

12. In a 1-2-4 concrete mix using 6 1/2 gallons of water per batch, the material that is used in the SMALLEST quantity is

    A. sand    B. cement    C. water    D. gravel

    12.____

13. It is specified that a concrete pavement be laid over a base of 5" of cinders. The BEST reason for this is that the

    A. cinders act as a binder between the earth and the concrete
    B. cinders aid in carrying off sub-surface drainage
    C. cinders offer a firm base, thereby minimizing the possibility of hollows and ridges
    D. use of cinders reduces the amount of cement required

    13.____

14. A supervisor should know what type of material has been covered in an employee training program. Of the following, the MOST important reason for this is that the supervisor

    A. can learn of any new developments or changes in work procedures
    B. can know more about his men's qualifications when making assignments
    C. can show his interest in the program and thus encourage his men to be more productive
    D. will know what training has not been covered and should be recommended for a future training program

    14.____

15. As soon as plant materials arrive from a nursery, they should be heeled in. Doing this will    15.__

    A. prevent root growth until the plant is transplanted
    B. keep the soil in better condition
    C. prevent drying out of the roots
    D. make certain that leaves and branches are not crushed

16. If a foreman determines that he cannot meet the deadline on a certain written report that    16.__
    his supervisor has assigned to him, he should

    A. work to the deadline and then ask for an extension
    B. inform his supervisor of his difficulty before the deadline
    C. ask another foreman for assistance
    D. meet the deadline even if he has to submit an inadequate report

17. After a heavy snow and sleet storm, the FIRST job of a park foreman is to see that    17.__

    A. walks of his section are cleared and sanded
    B. any damage to trees and buildings in his section is noted
    C. he gets instructions from the general park foreman
    D. ice skating areas are cleared of loose snow and properly planed

18. In planning winter maintenance of parks, the task which merits LEAST attention is    18.__

    A. sanding and salting of icy walks
    B. removal of snow from newly-seeded lawn areas
    C. keeping catch basin inlets clear during winter thaws
    D. checking equipment and supplies required for winter maintenance

19. Suppose that a person appears at the tennis courts and asks for an appointment to play.    19.__
    He does not have his tennis permit with him. However, you recognize him since he
    played the previous day and did possess a permit then. Your action should be to

    A. accept him because he has paid the required fee and is, therefore, eligible to play
    B. deny him admittance because he probably has given his card to another person
    C. deny him admittance because only permit holders may play on courts requiring
       permits
    D. accept his request for an appointment if he promises to show his card to you within
       the week

20. To reduce possible vandalism in parks, the park supervisor should    20.__

    A. inform his employees to break up any groups of children who are not engaged in
       play activities
    B. have his employees search all youths who may possess knives or other tools used
       by vandals
    C. instruct his men to make frequent regular tours of their areas
    D. instruct his men to concentrate on vandalism prevention rather than the routine
       maintenance of their areas

21. Supervisors should instruct their subordinates in the proper procedure for the maintenance and display of the National flag from flagpoles. These instructions should provide that

    A. on Memorial Day the flag be flown at half mast until sunset
    B. the flag be hoisted slowly and not be allowed to touch the ground
    C. when renewing a halyard care should be taken that the old halyard is completely removed before the new one is strung through the pulley
    D. when the flag is to be flown at half mast it should be hoisted briskly to the peak before being lowered to half staff

22. Suppose that a woman complains to you that one of your men was abusive when told there was a flooded condition in a comfort station. Your FIRST action on this complaint should be to

    A. tell the general park foreman about the complaint and recommend punitive action
    B. inform the complainant that the employee would have his assignment changed
    C. inform the complainant that the employee would be spoken to and the flooded condition corrected
    D. tell the complainant that she was probably wrong since park employees are instructed to be courteous and cooperative

23. Suppose that a newly assigned temporary assistant gardener is found sleeping on a park bench after his scheduled lunch hour. He offers no excuse other than his sleepiness after lunch. The MOST appropriate action in this situation is to

    A. warn him not to repeat this apparent neglect of duties
    B. determine his efficiency by inspecting the area he was supposed to rake and clean
    C. send him home for the day after warning him that a temporary employee ought to watch his step
    D. question him further about his neglect of duties since he may not know how to perform his assignment

24. Suppose that you notice that there is chronic non-observance of a posted sign warning persons to stay off a lawn which has been recently reseeded. Your men are unable to enforce the notice by speaking to the violators. Your next step should be to

    A. issue an order that violators be forcibly removed from the lawn
    B. order the arrest of any violators who are adults and can understand the meaning of the sign
    C. prepare a report for your general park foreman recommending that all violators be summoned to court
    D. inform the general park foreman of the situation so that he can recommend appropriate police action

25. Suppose that you saw two men with revolvers robbing another person in a small park. The MOST advisable thing for you to do is

    A. apprehend the robbers and bring them to the nearest police station
    B. get in touch with the general park foreman to have him report the occurrence to the borough office for appropriate police action
    C. seek police assistance immediately
    D. call out to the robbers, warning them to desist from robbing persons in a public park

26. Suppose that you are instructing your men on safety pre-cautions to be observed by them. Of the following, a precaution that should be followed is

   A. lye may be used to clean paint brushes, but must be carefully handled so that the hands do not touch it
   B. in using a file, the user should wear gloves to protect his hand from the sharp end of the file
   C. when using steel wool, gloves should be worn or hands otherwise protected
   D. chisels before being used should be mushroomed

27. A person in a playground shows symptoms of sunstroke and suddenly loses consciousness. Of the following steps in the aid of this person, the one that is NOT correct is

   A. call a doctor immediately
   B. apply cold wet cloths to person's head
   C. give stimulants such as cold water, spirits of ammonia or coffee
   D. remove some of the person's clothing, if possible

28. A child slips on the entrance step of a comfort station and injures herself. The next day, a lawyer representing the child's family asks you for information concerning the accident. You should

   A. be cooperative, showing the lawyer a copy of the accident report and discussing the condition of the comfort station
   B. tell the lawyer that the consent of the parents will be necessary before he releases any information
   C. refuse to answer any questions asked by the lawyer concerning the park or accident
   D. refer the lawyer to the borough office for further information about the accident

29. To provide for at least the minimum of care in a playground where the assigned employee is ill for a day, the park foreman should

   A. ask his supervisor to request an additional employee from central headquarters to cover the playground during this period
   B. assign the least competent employee to cover this playground in addition to his regular assignment for disciplinary purposes
   C. have all his employees take turns in covering the playground during the day
   D. have his most reliable employee cover the playground for the day

30. When a park supervisor is assigned to a new section, it is his responsibility and duty to lay out and schedule the performance of the work in his section so that the proper standard of operation is obtained. In preparing the schedule of maintenance, the FIRST step the park supervisor should take is to

   A. observe the men at work in his section to determine personnel replacement needs
   B. determine the exact area of his section
   C. learn the number of employees assigned to the section
   D. determine the amount of work required in the parks and playgrounds of his section

31. Competent supervision of work includes the laying out of the sequence of operations to be performed by employees so that there is a minimum of lost time and the work is performed in an efficient manner. To carry out this phase of supervision, the park supervisor should

    A. refer to the superintendent all instances where laborers fail to follow out the specific instructions given by him
    B. discuss with his laborers the job he wants done before assigning them to do the job
    C. watch his laborers and other subordinates continuously to make certain that they work efficiently
    D. assign an efficient employee along with an inefficient employee to see that the required work is completed

31.____

32. A factor that merits LEAST consideration in the periodic ordering of maintenance supplies and equipment is

    A. number and types of playgrounds in the section
    B. number of employees assigned to the section
    C. condition and type of play area surfaces in the section
    D. extent to which play areas in the section have been used

32.____

33. An employee requests supplies which are not standard items. The park supervisor should handle this request by

    A. refusing to forward the requisition because the supplies are probably not needed
    B. refusing to order the supplies unless urgently needed
    C. having the employee explain his request to determine whether standard items might be ordered instead
    D. reviewing carefully the work habits of the employee since the request is unusual and does not follow standard procedure

33.____

34. To determine the efficiency of an employee assigned in charge of a playground, the MOST important guide is the

    A. amount of cleaning material used during the year
    B. attendance record during the year
    C. number of required repairs to playground surfaces and walks during the year
    D. appearance of the playground during the year

34.____

35. Two part-time rink attendants earn $6,240 and $6,220 per annum, respectively, exclusive of a bonus of $2,640 per annum. If both have a pension deduction of 20%, the difference in the pension deduction of the two attendants on a semi-monthly basis is

    A. $1.50    B. $.50    C. $1.00    D. $.25

35.____

36. Suppose you are asked to prepare service rating reports on your subordinates. A fact which would NOT be reported on the service rating form is

    A. length of time employee has worked in your section
    B. excessive lateness or absence
    C. length of time employee has been employed in the Department
    D. exact title of employee

36.____

37. With respect to a concession in his park, the park supervisor should see that the

    A. area within fifty feet of the concession is maintained in a clean condition by the concessionaire
    B. concession is not operated on Sundays unless specifically permitted by the general park foreman
    C. concession or a carretina is not located within fifty feet of a comfort station
    D. employees of the concessionaire are at least 18 years of age and are suffering from no communicable disease

38. Of the following, the statement that is MOST correct with respect to the maintenance of hedges is that

    A. hedges should be clipped in the winter or early spring before any growth begins
    B. hedges should not be trimmed at all until late summer after secondary growth occurs
    C. annual clipping of privet hedges should be done just after the first strong growth has slowed down
    D. flat tops are preferred to rounded tops because snow is shed more easily by flat tops

39. In general, parkway maintenance is LEAST dependent on the

    A. frequency of use of benches and paths
    B. types of trees planted along the parkway
    C. neighborhoods through which the parkway runs
    D. amount and kind of traffic

40. Of the following, the MOST important reason for the construction of marginal playgrounds in large parks is to

    A. reduce damage to lawns and landscaped areas by children
    B. permit installation of modern playground equipment in space specifically designed for its use
    C. increase the area available for open field sports
    D. reduce the cost of playground operation and maintenance

# KEY (CORRECT ANSWERS)

| | | | |
|---|---|---|---|
| 1. A | 11. B | 21. D | 31. B |
| 2. D | 12. C | 22. C | 32. B |
| 3. C | 13. B | 23. A | 33. C |
| 4. C | 14. B | 24. D | 34. D |
| 5. D | 15. C | 25. C | 35. D |
| 6. C | 16. B | 26. C | 36. C |
| 7. D | 17. A | 27. C | 37. A |
| 8. B | 18. B | 28. D | 38. C |
| 9. A | 19. C | 29. D | 39. B |
| 10. B | 20. C | 30. D | 40. A |

# EXAMINATION SECTION
# TEST 1

DIRECTIONS: Each question or incomplete statement is followed by several suggested answers or completions. Select the one that BEST answers the question or completes the statement. *PRINT THE LETTER OF THE CORRECT ANSWER IN THE SPACE AT THE RIGHT.*

1. Of the following, the MOST valuable and desirable trait in a supervisor is a(n)    1.____

    A. ability to get the best work out of his men
    B. ability to inspire his men with the desire to *get ahead in the world*
    C. persuasive manner of speech
    D. tall and commanding appearance

2. The park supervisor who is MOST suitable for the general practical needs of the park department is the one who    2.____

    A. gets a great deal of satisfactory work done although usually handicapped by constant bickering among his subordinates
    B. gets a great deal of satisfactory work done because of his ability to do a large amount of it himself
    C. gets less work done than the other supervisors but has unusually high quality work production standards
    D. gets more than an average amount of satisfactory work done because of the cooperative way in which the men work for him

3. A park supervisor has been transferred to a new section. The BEST way for him to get cooperation from his subordinates would be to    3.____

    A. ask the superintendent to give him strong support
    B. explain his policy firmly so that the men cannot blame him for any mistakes made
    C. note the troublemakers and have them transferred out
    D. show his men that he not only is interested in getting work done but also has their welfare in mind

4. A knowledge of the experience and abilities of the subordinates working under him is MOST useful to a supervisor in    4.____

    A. deciding what type of discipline to exercise when necessary
    B. finding the cause of minor accidents on the job
    C. making proper work assignments
    D. making vacation schedules

5. A supervisor will be able to train his subordinates better if he is familiar with basic principles of learning. Which one of the following statements about the learning process is MOST correct?    5.____

    A. A subordinate who learns one job quickly will learn any other job quickly.
    B. Emphasizing correct things done by the subordinate usually gives him an incentive to improve.
    C. Great importance placed on a subordinate's mistakes is the best way to help him to get rid of them.
    D. It is very hard to teach new methods to middle-aged or older subordinates.

6. Several experienced employees have resigned. You have decided to arrange for permanent transfers of other experienced employees in your section to fill their jobs, leaving only jobs that new, inexperienced employees can fill easily. For you, the park supervisor, to talk this over with the employees who will be affected by the move would be

    A. *bad;* it would show weakness and wavering by you
    B. *bad;* transfers should be made on the basis of efficiency
    C. *good;* it will help you get better cooperation from the employees involved
    D. *good;* transfer should be made on the basis of seniority

7. An assistant gardener under your supervision does much less work than he is capable of. What should be your FIRST step in an effort to improve his performance?

    A. Discovering why he is not working up to his full capacity
    B. Going over his mistakes and shortcomings with him to reduce them
    C. Pointing out to him that the quality of his work is below standard
    D. Showing him that the other men produce much more than he does

8. The first thing a certain park supervisor does when he assigns a subordinate to a new job is to find out what the man already knows about the job. This practice is

    A. *good;* mainly because the subordinate may know more than the supervisor about the job
    B. *good;* mainly because this information will help the supervisor in instructing the subordinate
    C. *poor;* mainly because since it's a new job the subordinate can't be expected to know anything
    D. *poor;* mainly because the supervisor should first find out how the subordinate will feel toward the job

9. Jones and Smith, who work together, do slightly more than an average amount of work for two men together. But you find that Jones does most of the work while Smith does less than he should. To correct this situation, the BEST thing for you as supervisor to do would be to

    A. assign work to Smith for which he must be personally responsible
    B. make a complaint to the superintendent about Smith, but praise Jones
    C. point out to Jones that he does most of the work and that he should urge Smith to do more
    D. require Smith to do more whenever the work of both men altogether falls below the expected average

10. You have given a new subordinate detailed instructions on how he should do a job. When you return a little later you find that the subordinate was afraid to start the job because he did not completely understand your instructions. In this situation, it would be BEST for you to

    A. assign the subordinate to a job where less intelligence is needed
    B. explain again, illustrating if possible how the job is to be done
    C. explain again, and recommend him for dropping at the end of probation if he does not understand
    D. make the subordinate explain why he did not at least start the job

11. A gardener does very good work but he has trouble getting to work on time. To get the man to come on time, the supervisor should

    A. bring him up on charges to stop the lateness once and for all
    B. have him report to the superintendent every time he is late
    C. talk over the problem with him to find its cause and possible solution
    D. threaten to transfer him if he cannot get to work early

12. As supervisor, you observe that an assistant gardener keeps making mistakes. Of the following, the BEST thing for you to do would be to

    A. make no mention of these mistakes as they gradually disappear with experience
    B. point the mistakes out to this man in front of the other subordinates so all may learn from them
    C. talk to the man privately about these mistakes and show him how to avoid them
    D. try to transfer this man out in exchange for a subordinate who can do the work

13. Proper action by the supervisor could MOST probably prevent work delays in his section caused by

    A. a large number of subordinates quitting their jobs in the park department
    B. the daily assignments of the subordinates not being properly planned
    C. the inexperience of new subordinates transferred into his section
    D. unexpected delays in delivery of material

14. If, after careful thought, you have definitely decided that one of your subordinates should be disciplined, it is MOST important for you to realize that

    A. discipline is the best tool for leading subordinates
    B. discipline should be severe in order to get the best results
    C. the discipline should be delayed so that its full force can be felt
    D. the subordinate should know why he is being disciplined

15. Your superior has sent to you for planting in your section a type of shrubbery which, in your opinion, is not suitable for the area. In this situation, it would be BEST for you to

    A. plant the shrubbery since your superior is responsible
    B. send the shrubbery back and ask for material suitable for the area
    C. talk it over with the subordinates under you to see if they think as you do
    D. talk the matter over with your superior right away

16. In repairing a crack in concrete, it is important to

    A. keep the patch dry until it hardens
    B. level the patch with the old surface while the concrete is quite wet
    C. smooth the edges of the crack before filling
    D. wet the old concrete surface when applying a patch

17. A usual method of *curing* concrete is to

    A. add common salt
    B. expose it to the sun
    C. keep it damp
    D. mix it for the proper period of time

18. Which one of the following statements about the operation of the steam heating system of a building is NOT correct?

    A. A disadvantage of draining the boiler each heating season is that air is admitted when the boiler is refilled.
    B. Hammering in the steam pipes indicates interference with the circulation of the water.
    C. Proper operation of radiator air-vent valves is indicated when steam escapes continuously from the valves.
    D. Rising level of water in the boiler may indicate a worn washer in the valve admitting water to the boiler

19. A smoking chimney connected to an oil burner system may indicate a(n)

    A. clogged chimney
    B. oversupply of air
    C. undersupply of air
    D. undersupply of oil

20. As compared to brass pipe, copper tubing has the advantage of

    A. being a lot cheaper
    B. being more flexible
    C. having a smooth surface
    D. requiring no special fittings

21. An air cushion in a water plumbing system will

    A. confine sewer gas
    B. increase water pressure
    C. prevent chattering when the faucet is partly open
    D. prevent water hammer

22. A short piece of pipe threaded on the outside at both ends is usually called a

    A. coupling    B. nipple    C. joint    D. union

23. The MOST important purpose of a trap placed in a wasteline beneath a sink is to

    A. block sewer gas
    B. catch dirt
    C. provide a cleanout
    D. provide venting

24. The one of the following which has the same purpose as a fuse in an electrical system is a

    A. circuit breaker
    B. condenser
    C. relay
    D. transformer

25. New galvanized iron fixtures are BEST prepared for painting by

    A. cleaning with steel wool
    B. finishing with emery cloth
    C. scouring with cleanser powder
    D. washing with vinegar solution

# KEY (CORRECT ANSWERS)

1. A
2. D
3. D
4. C
5. B

6. C
7. A
8. B
9. A
10. B

11. C
12. C
13. B
14. D
15. D

16. D
17. C
18. C
19. C
20. B

21. D
22. B
23. A
24. A
25. D

# TEST 2

DIRECTIONS: Each question or incomplete statement is followed by several suggested answers or completions. Select the one that BEST answers the question or completes the statement. *PRINT THE LETTER OF THE CORRECT ANSWER IN THE SPACE AT THE RIGHT.*

1. Blistering of paint on an outside wall is MOST likely to be caused by too       1.___

    A. little sunlight hitting the wall
    B. much moisture from inside the building
    C. much moisture from outside the building
    D. much sunlight hitting the wall

2. Which of the following is MOST likely to be caused by putting a hard finish coat of paint over a soft primer?       2.___

    A. Alligatoring           B. Chalking
    C. Flaking                D. Wrinkling

3. For cleaning shellac from a brush, it is BEST to use       3.___

    A. benzine               B. denatured alcohol
    C. lacquer thinner       D. turpentine

4. Emery cloth is usually used as a(n)       4.___

    A. mulch                 B. abrasive
    C. pipe covering         D. waterproof covering

5. To remove dirt spots from asphalt floor tile, it is BEST to use       5.___

    A. benzine               B. carbon tetrachloride
    C. soap and water        D. turpentine

6. A carbide tipped drill is ordinarily required for drilling in       6.___

    A. aluminum              B. cast iron
    C. hard steel            D. masonry

7. A toggle bolt is usually MOST suitable for attaching objects to       7.___

    A. hollow masonry        B. thick brick walls
    C. thick concrete walls  D. studs or beams

8. Authorities on park maintenance often recommend that large picnic tables be anchored to the ground. The MAIN reason given is that such anchoring       8.___

    A. keeps the picnic tables in even rows
    B. prevents damage caused by moving
    C. prevents theft by the public
    D. restricts picnicking to picnic grounds

9. Calcium chloride is useful on a tennis court for       9.___

    A. keeping dust down             B. keeping the surface packed down
    C. marking the court             D. reflecting the heat

10. The MAIN reason a fireplace built with a chimney is NOT recommended for picnic areas at beaches and parks is that such fireplaces  10.____

    A. are hard to maintain
    B. cost so much to construct
    C. increase the danger of fire
    D. provide too much draft

11. The type of outdoor fireplace which is MOST economical and easiest to maintain is  11.____

    A. an entirely concrete fireplace
    B. an upright steel charcoal burner
    C. one made of cement mixed with asbestos
    D. one made of masonry lined with firebrick

12. Copper sulphate is MOST likely to be used in the operation of a swimming pool  12.____

    A. as a paint
    B. as a water softener
    C. for control of algae
    D. for filtering the water

13. The inspection of a wading pool to determine if it is in good condition does NOT usually include a check of  13.____

    A. expansion joints for tightness
    B. foots at base of fence for lead
    C. porous blocks for drainage
    D. valve pit for debris

14. A program of preventive maintenance for equipment which includes periodic inspection and upkeep is MOST likely to result in  14.____

    A. fewer large scale repairs because repairs can be made before they become more serious
    B. higher labor costs for repairs since single repairs rather than an accumulation of repairs are made at one time
    C. less total productive time from each piece of equipment because of the periodic removal from service
    D. the need for more standby equipment to replace equipment taken out of service

15. The one of the following which will probably contribute MOST to keeping park areas in a clean and orderly condition is a  15.____

    A. large number of receptacles for refuse
    B. large number of signs strategically placed
    C. distribution of park department rules and regulations to park users
    D. spirit of cooperation on the part of the public

16. The addition of organic matter to the soil is  16.____

    A. good for both clay soils and for sandy soils
    B. good for clay soils but not for sandy soils
    C. good for sandy soils but not for clay soils
    D. not recommended for dry soils

17. Animal manure should usually be added to the soil when the manure is    17.____

    A. completely dried out
    B. not yet rotted
    C. partially rotted
    D. sure to come in contact with plant roots

18. Which one of these materials is organic?    18.____

    A. Lime            B. Muriate of potash
    C. Peat            D. Superphosphate

19. The three plant food elements which are usually NOT present in the soil in sufficient    19.____
    amounts needed by plants are

    A. nitrogen, calcium, sulphur
    B. nitrogen, phosphorus, potassium
    C. phosphorus, hydrogen, carbon
    D. potassium, magnesium, sulphur

20. A change in the pH of a soil from 6.5 to 7.5 indicates that the soil    20.____

    A. has a greater moisture content
    B. has become neutral
    C. is more acid
    D. is more alkaline

21. An acid soil is indicated if upon contact with the soil _____ litmus paper turns _____.    21.____

    A. blue; purple       B. blue; red
    C. red; blue          D. red; purple

22. Of the following, the MOST correct statement about fertilizers is that    22.____

    A. a fertilizer may consist of a single plant food element or of a combination of several plant food elements
    B. an inorganic fertilizer is made up of natural plant foods such as decomposed vegetable and animal substances
    C. an organic fertilizer is one produced commercially out of a combination of various chemicals
    D. the purpose of fertilizers is to kill insect pests as well as to feed plants

23. A bag of 10-6-4 fertilizer contains    23.____

    A. 10 percent nitrogen       B. 4 percent phosphorus
    C. 10 percent potash         D. 6 percent nitrogen

24. Which of these is a temporary grass?    24.____

    A. Creeping bent             B. Creeping red fescue
    C. Kentucky bluegrass        D. Redtop

25. An established lawn should usually be rolled one or two times, _____, in the _____.    25.____

    A. heavily; fall             B. heavily; summer
    C. lightly; fall             D. lightly; spring

# KEY (CORRECT ANSWERS)

| | | | |
|---|---|---|---|
| 1. | C | 11. | B |
| 2. | A | 12. | C |
| 3. | B | 13. | C |
| 4. | B | 14. | A |
| 5. | C | 15. | D |
| 6. | D | 16. | A |
| 7. | A | 17. | C |
| 8. | B | 18. | C |
| 9. | A | 19. | B |
| 10. | D | 20. | D |

21. B
22. A
23. A
24. D
25. D

# TEST 3

DIRECTIONS: Each question or incomplete statement is followed by several suggested answers or completions. Select the one that BEST answers the question or completes the statement. *PRINT THE LETTER OF THE CORRECT ANSWER IN THE SPACE AT THE RIGHT.*

1. As compared with other grasses, common Bermuda grass has the DISADVANTAGE that it                                  1._____

    A. can easily crowd out other desirable plants
    B. cannot stand intense summer heat
    C. cannot stand much wear
    D. is particularly subject to pests and diseases

2. After a new lawn is seeded, it should be                                  2._____

    A. covered with at least 1/4 inch of soil
    B. kept moist until the grass is well up
    C. raked lightly for several days
    D. watered with a heavy spray

3. Frequent light watering of lawns is MOST likely to                                  3._____

    A. cause erosion
    B. prevent fungus diseases
    C. result in a dense luxuriant turf
    D. result in shallow root systems

4. The one of the following which is suitable for use against crab grass in a lawn is                                  4._____

    A. DDT                    B. lindane
    C. potassium cyanate      D. 2, 4-D

5. In the maintenance of an established lawn, it is NOT considered good practice to                                  5._____

    A. fertilize in hot and dry summer weather
    B. leave lawn clippings on the ground
    C. remove fallen leaves from the lawn
    D. water thoroughly during dry spells

6. Plugs are                                  6._____

    A. a type of grass seed
    B. grass roots cut into bits
    C. small circular cuts of sod
    D. small sprigs of grass

7. The MAIN chemical ingredients in bordeaux mixture are                                  7._____

    A. copper sulphate and lime
    B. copper sulphate and sulphur
    C. nicotine sulphate and copper
    D. sulphur and lime

8. Privet planted as hedge material should usually be set about _____ inches apart.

   A. 3  B. 9  C. 18  D. 24

9. A hedge should be cut so that it is narrower at the top than at the bottom. This practice is

   A. *bad;* it does not let sunlight get to the base of the hedge
   B. *bad;* it stunts the growth of the hedge
   C. *good;* it is done to allow sunlight to get to the lower leaves
   D. *good;* it is done to speed up growth

10. The transplanting of deciduous trees in full leaf is not recommended, but it may be done successfully if the whole plant is sprayed with special plastic to cover both sides of the leaves. The MOST important reason for the success of such a practice is that it helps

    A. preserve the bark
    B. preserve the leaves
    C. prevent sun scald
    D. prevent water loss

11. If a tree is to be transplanted from its natural habitat, it is desirable to root prune it at least one growing season in advance MAINLY in order to

    A. increase its resistance to disease
    B. induce growth of new roots in a fibrous mass
    C. reduce its requirements for moisture and nutrients
    D. reduce top growth

12. The top of a deciduous tree is often cut back severely when the tree is transplanted bare rooted. The MAIN purpose of this cutting back is to

    A. allow sun to get at the bark
    B. help the tree withstand the wind
    C. make it easier to move the tree
    D. make up for root loss

13. Of the following trees, the one which grows BEST in the east coast is the

    A. ginkgo  B. larch  C. sour gum  D. sweet gum

14. Which of these is an evergreen?

    A. American elm
    B. Honey locust
    C. Norway maple
    D. Weeping hemlock

15. It is recommended that a shrub which bears blossoms on last year's wood be pruned soon after it has bloomed. This recommendation is

    A. *bad,* because pruning should not be done during a period of very active growth
    B. *bad,* because such pruning should not be done when the plant is in a weakened condition
    C. *good,* because such pruning helps the plant put its energy into desirable growth
    D. *good,* because then the pruning is done when the plant is least exposed to disease

Questions 16-19.

DIRECTIONS: Questions 16 through 19 are to be answered on the basis of the paragraph given below. Your answers to these questions must be based only on the information given in this paragraph.

Maintenance of leased or licensed areas on public parks or lands has always been a problem. A good rule to follow in the administration and maintenance of such areas is to limit the responsibility of any lessee or licensee to the maintenance of the structures and grounds essential to the efficient operation of the concession, not including areas for the general use of the public, such as picnic areas, public comfort stations, etc., except where such facilities are leased to another public agency or where special conditions make such inclusion practicable, and where a good standard of maintenance can be assured and enforced. If local conditions and requirements are such that public use areas are included, adequate safeguards to the public should be written into contracts and enforced in their administration, to insure that maintenance by the concessionaire shall be equal to the maintenance standards for other park property.

16. According to the above paragraph, when an area on a public park is leased to a concessionaire, it is usually BEST to 16.___

    A. confine the responsibility of the concessionaire to operation of the facilities and leave the maintenance function to the park agency
    B. exclude areas of general public use from the maintenance obligation of the concessionaire
    C. make the concessionaire responsible for maintenance of the entire area, including areas of general public use
    D. provide additional comfort station facilities for the area

17. According to the above paragraph, a valid reason for giving a concessionaire responsibility for maintenance of a picnic area within his leased area is that 17.___

    A. local conditions and requirements made it practicable
    B. more than half of the picnic area falls within his leased area
    C. the concessionaire has leased picnic facilities to another public agency
    D. the picnic area falls entirely within his leased area

18. According to the above paragraph, a precaution that should be taken when a concessionaire is made responsible for maintenance of an area of general public use in a park is 18.___

    A. making sure that another public agency has not previously been made responsible for this area
    B. providing the concessionaire with up-to-date equipment, if practicable
    C. requiring that the concessionaire take out adequate insurance for the protection of the public
    D. writing safeguards to the public into the contract

19. According to the above paragraph, the level of maintenance performed by a concessionaire on an area of general public use for which he is responsible should be   19.____

    A. equal to standards for other park property only if special conditions make this practicable
    B. equivalent to that on any other public property
    C. equivalent to that on other areas of the park
    D. higher than in other surrounding areas

Questions 20-23.

DIRECTIONS: Questions 20 through 23 refer to the sprayer described in the following paragraph.

This is a hydraulic, power wheelbarrow sprayer with a tank capacity of 20 gallons. It is equipped with piston type pumps which deliver at maximum 1.5 gpm. Power is furnished by a small air-cooled engine.

20. The sprayer described in the above paragraph is MOST likely to be used for   20.____

    A. sanitation spraying
    B. spraying small lawns and shrubs
    C. spraying tall shade trees
    D. treating large areas for mosquito control

21. The word *hydraulic* used to describe this sprayer indicates MOST probably that   21.____

    A. compressed air carries the particles of spray
    B. liquid pressure plays an important part in the operation of the sprayer
    C. oil is an important part of the mixture sprayed
    D. the mixture which is sprayed has a high percentage of water

22. The piston in the pump described in the above paragraph is probably MOST NEARLY like a   22.____

    A. gear                 B. hollow open tube
    C. solid cylinder       D. wheel

23. If the sprayer described above used up the complete contents of a full tank in 16 minutes, it would be delivering at less than its maximum rate by _____ gallon per minute.   23.____

    A. 3/4      B. 1/2      C. 1/6      D. 1/4

24. The MAIN reason why a park supervisor should be familiar with the principles and practices of report writing is that he   24.____

    A. can then understand the reports issued by the Department better
    B. might be promoted to an administrative position
    C. must be able to write a report if an emergency should occur
    D. must submit reports in connection with his work

25. Of the following, the BEST reason why a park supervisor should prepare a report on an unusual incident as soon as possible after it happens is that

    A. he might forget some of the facts if he waits
    B. he might not have time to do so later on
    C. this gives his supervisor the opportunity to review his report before anyone else sees it
    D. this proves that he was on the job

---

# KEY (CORRECT ANSWERS)

| | | | |
|---|---|---|---|
| 1. | A | 11. | B |
| 2. | B | 12. | D |
| 3. | D | 13. | A |
| 4. | C | 14. | D |
| 5. | A | 15. | C |
| 6. | C | 16. | B |
| 7. | B | 17. | A |
| 8. | B | 18. | D |
| 9. | C | 19. | C |
| 10. | D | 20. | B |

21. B
22. C
23. D
24. D
25. A

# TEST 4

DIRECTIONS: Each question or incomplete statement is followed by several suggested answers or completions. Select the one that BEST answers the question or completes the statement. *PRINT THE LETTER OF THE CORRECT ANSWER IN THE SPACE AT THE RIGHT.*

1. The FIRST step usually taken in writing a report is to

    A. decide how long the report should be
    B. determine how many copies of the report will be needed
    C. determine what is to be included in the report
    D. read copies of other reports of a similar nature

    1.____

2. The introduction or beginning of a report on a certain procedure in an organization usually should NOT contain

    A. a brief statement of the conclusions reached
    B. a statement of the subject of the report
    C. examples of procedures in other organizations
    D. the reason for the report

    2.____

3. An example of a periodic report is a(n)

    A. monthly activities report
    B. accident report
    C. probationary report on an employee
    D. report on the effectiveness of a new procedure

    3.____

4. The one of the following which is NOT an important reason for requiring a complete report of an accident is that

    A. employees should receive proper training in the writing of complete reports
    B. it is desirable to have a full record of all accidents
    C. the report can be used as a basis for determining the cause of the accident
    D. the report can be used as a basis for eliminating the cause of such accidents in the future

    4.____

5. A vandalism report on damage to a certain comfort station states: *The copper metal lining the intersection of chimney with roof was completely cut away.* Too many words are used in this report to describe the

    A. eaves trough          B. flashing
    C. wainscoting           D. weather stripping

    5.____

6. Which of the following is prohibited in a park, without exception, by the rules and regulations of the department of parks?

    A. Capturing a pigeon
    B. Feeding popcorn to squirrels
    C. Kindling a wood fire
    D. Remaining after 12:00 midnight

    6.____

7. According to the rules and regulations of the department of parks, a licensed ambulance on emergency service using a parkway under the jurisdiction of the department is    7.____

   A. not permitted to sound its siren unless there is a traffic jam
   B. permitted to exceed the maximum speed limit prescribed for other vehicles
   C. subject to all traffic regulations for other vehicles
   D. to be given the right of way by other vehicles

8. According to the rules and regulations of the department of parks, a motorist who gets a flat tire on an improved or paved park roadway must    8.____

   A. continue slowly to a point beyond the nearest park exit where he may then change the tire
   B. get the vehicle completely off the roadway in order to remove and replace the tire
   C. have the vehicle towed to the nearest exit by a tow truck which has a permit issued by the Commissioner of Parks
   D. put a person or warning device seventy feet to the rear of the vehicle while making repairs on the roadway

9. With respect to permits issued to carry on any activity in a park, it is MOST correct to state that    9.____

   A. permits are not required for organized picnics or outings
   B. permits for the use of parks in which there is located a botanical or zoological society require the approval of the society
   C. the permit will not be issued if it is desired for the purpose of conducting an affair of a private or commercial nature
   D. when the permit is revoked, the fee must be refunded

10. The preferred minimum distance from the ground for the lowest limb of a tree in a park playground is _____ feet.    10.____

    A. 5          B. 6          C. 7          D. 8

11. The permit for digging a hole to plant a street tree in a borough is issued by the    11.____

    A. Director
    B. Office of the County Executive
    C. Department of Highways
    D. Senior Horticulturist of the Department of Parks

12. In playgrounds operated jointly by the department of parks and the board of education, the board of education is USUALLY responsible for    12.____

    A. their maintenance
    B. their operation during school hours, except for areas set aside for mothers and pre-school age children
    C. their operation during the summer and weekends, except for areas set aside for mothers and pre-school age children
    D. the supervision of the kindergarten section at all times

3 (#4)

13. If a new maintenance procedure has been adopted, the supervisor should keep this work under his close super vision until the procedure has become routine. Of the following, the MOST important reason for doing this is to      13.____

    A. impress the workers with the importance of the job
    B. get the work done as quickly as possible
    C. make certain that the workers are following the procedure correctly
    D. find out how long the job should take

14. Assume that a supervisor is preparing a report recommending that a standard work procedure be changed.      14.____
    Of the following, the MOST important information that he should include in this report is

    A. the type and amount of re-training that will be needed
    B. a complete description of the present procedure
    C. the opinion of his supervisor
    D. the details and advantages of the recommended procedure

15. A supervisor tells a maintainer to make certain changes on a job which the maintainer has just completed. The maintainer tells the supervisor that he feels the changes are not necessary.      15.____
    The supervisor should

    A. leave the job as it is and explain to his supervisor why the changes were not made
    B. save time by having another maintainer make the changes
    C. explain why the changes are to be made and insist this maintainer do it
    D. arrange a meeting for this maintainer with the supervisor's supervisor

16. When a ladder is used in working against the side of a building, for safest operation the base of the ladder should be placed at a distance from the building equal to APPROXIMATELY _____ the length of the ladder.      16.____

    A. 1/2        B. 1/3        C. 1/4        D. 1/5

17. Workers should not be allowed to work from ladders footed on open trucks. The MAIN reason for this is that the      17.____

    A. floor of a truck is not level
    B. floor of a truck is usually slippery
    C. truck might move unexpectedly
    D. truck might be scratched or otherwise damaged

18. The mist blower or concentrate sprayer is used MAINLY for      18.____

    A. application of liquid fertilizers
    B. control of grass, brush, or forest fires
    C. fly and mosquito control
    D. shade tree work

19. Of the following, the MOST satisfactory type of spade is one made with a      19.____

    A. heavy handle
    B. metal shank which extends part way up the handle

C. plastic handle
D. single sheet of metal pressed into shape

20. Portable generators are ideal for operating portable tools. The generator referred to in this statement is  20.____

   A. a type of battery
   B. a type of motor
   C. used for changing electrical energy into mechanical energy
   D. used for changing mechanical energy into electrical energy

21. Chains on a lawnmower work longer and better when they are  21.____

   A. lubricated once each year
   B. lubricated twice each year
   C. lubricated weekly and more frequently if necessary
   D. not lubricated

22. Of the following pieces of equipment, the one which is MOST efficient for mowing tall, coarse, tough grass is a large  22.____

   A. brush chipper             B. reel mower
   C. rotary mower              D. sickle bar mower

23. With spark plug out, hold thumb over spark plug hole while engine is rotated. When compression is felt, replace spark plug. This one step is recommended in preparation of a gasoline-driven lawnmower for winter storage. The MAIN reason such a step is taken is to  23.____

   A. avoid sticking of the valves later
   B. insure proper timing of valves later
   C. make sure valves are open
   D. put tension on the valves

24. A standard recommendation for operating a gasoline-driven mower is that the motor should warm up before the mower is put to use. The MAIN reason for this is to get the  24.____

   A. engine broken in before it carries any load
   B. proper clearance and lubrication for moving parts
   C. proper gas-air mixture at the carburetor
   D. proper timing for spark plug firing

25. Treat a running engine-driven rotary mower as you would a gun. This warning is MOST probably justified because  25.____

   A. objects flying from the mower blades can cause injury
   B. such mowers are, and should be, treated like precision instruments
   C. the mower should be treated with the care of a valued possession
   D. the mower should be well-oiled and housed

## KEY (CORRECT ANSWERS)

| | | | |
|---|---|---|---|
| 1. | C | 11. | B |
| 2. | C | 12. | B |
| 3. | A | 13. | C |
| 4. | A | 14. | D |
| 5. | B | 15. | C |
| 6. | A | 16. | C |
| 7. | C | 17. | C |
| 8. | B | 18. | D |
| 9. | C | 19. | B |
| 10. | D | 20. | D |

21. D
22. C
23. A
24. B
25. A

# EXAMINATION SECTION
# TEST 1

DIRECTIONS: Each question or incomplete statement is followed by several suggested answers or completions. Select the one that BEST answers the question or completes the statement. *PRINT THE LETTER OF THE CORRECT ANSWER IN THE SPACE AT THE RIGHT.*

1. Which of the following is the MOST likely action a supervisor should take to help establish an effective working relationship with his departmental superiors?
   A. Delay the implementation of new procedures received from superiors in order to evaluate their appropriateness.
   B. Skip the chain of command whenever he feels that it is to his advantage
   C. Keep supervisors informed of problems in his area and the steps taken to correct them
   D. Don't take up superiors' time by discussing anticipated problems but wait until the difficulties occur

    1.____

2. Of the following, the action a supervisor could take which would generally be MOST conducive to the establishment of an effective working relationship with employees includes
   A. maintaining impersonal relationships to prevent development of biased actions
   B. treating all employees equally without adjusting for individual differences
   C. continuous observation of employees on the job with insistence on constant improvement
   D. careful planning and scheduling of work for your employees

    2.____

3. Which of the following procedures is the LEAST likely to establish effective working relationships between employees and supervisors?
   A. Encouraging two-way communication with employees
   B. Periodic discussion with employees regarding their job performance
   C. Ignoring employees' gripes concerning job difficulties
   D. Avoiding personal prejudices in dealing with employees

    3.____

4. Criticism can be used as a tool to point out the weak areas of a subordinate's work performance.
   Of the following, the BEST action for a supervisor to take so that his criticism will be accepted is to
   A. focus his criticism on the act instead of on the person
   B. exaggerate the errors in order to motivate the employee to do better
   C. pass judgment quickly and privately without investigating the circumstances of the error
   D. generalize the criticism and not specifically point out the errors in performance

    4.____

2 (#1)

5. In trying to improve the motivation of his subordinates, a supervisor can achieve the BEST results by taking action based upon the assumption that most employees
   A. have an inherent dislike of work
   B. wish to be closely directed
   C. are more interested in security than in assuming responsibility
   D. will exercise self-direction without coercion

   5.____

6. When there are conflicts or tensions between top management and lower-level employees in any department, the supervisor should FIRST attempt to
   A. represent and enforce the management point of view
   B. act as the representative of the workers to get their ideas across to management
   C. serve as a two-way spokesman, trying to interpret each side to the other
   D. remain neutral, but keep informed of changes in the situation

   6.____

7. A probationary period for new employees is usually provided in many agencies. The MAJOR purpose of such a period is usually to
   A. allow a determination of employee's suitability for the position
   B. obtain evidence as to employee's ability to perform in a higher position
   C. conform to requirements that ethnic hiring goals be met for all positions
   D. train the new employee in the duties of the position

   7.____

8. An effective program of orientation for new employees usually includes all of the following EXCEPT
   A. having the supervisor introduce the new employee to his job, outlining his responsibilities and how to carry them out
   B. permitting the new worker to tour the facility or department so he can observe all parts of it in action
   C. scheduling meetings for new employees, at which the job requirements are explained to them and they are given personnel manuals
   D. testing the new worker on his skills and sending him to a centralized in-service workshop

   8.____

9. In-service training is an important responsibility of many supervisors. The MAJOR reason for such training is to
   A. avoid future grievance procedures because employees might say they were not prepared to carry out their jobs
   B. maximize the effectiveness of the department by helping each employee perform at his full potential
   C. satisfy inspection teams from central headquarters of the department
   D. help prevent disagreements with members of the community

   9.____

10. There are many forms of useful in-service training.
    Of the following, the training method which is NOT an appropriate technique for leadership development is to
    A. provide special workshops or clinics in activity skills
    B. conduct institutes to familiarize new workers with the program of the department and with their roles

    10.____

C. schedule team meetings for problem-solving, including both supervisors and leaders
D. have the leader rate himself on an evaluation form periodically

11. Of the following techniques of evaluating work training programs, the one that is BEST is to
    A. pass out a carefully designed questionnaire to the trainees at the completion of the program
    B. test the knowledge that trainees have both at the beginning of training and at its completion
    C. interview the trainees at the completion of the program
    D. evaluate performance before and after training for both a control group and an experimental group

11._____

12. Assume that a new supervisor is having difficulty making his instructions to subordinates clearly understood.
    The one of the following which is the FIRST step he should take in dealing with this problem is to
    A. set up a training workshop in communication skills
    B. determine the extent and nature of the communications gap
    C. repeat both verbal and written instructions several times
    D. simplify his written and spoken vocabulary

12._____

13. A director has not properly carried out the orders of his assistant supervisor on several occasions to the point where he has been successively warned, reprimanded, and severely reprimanded.
    When the director once again does not carry out orders, the PROPER action for the assistant supervisor to take is to
    A. bring the director up on charges of failing to perform his duties properly
    B. have a serious discussion with the director, explaining the need for the orders and the necessity for carrying them out
    C. recommend that the director be transferred to another district
    D. severely reprimand the director again, making clear that no further deviation will be countenanced

13._____

14. A supervisor with several subordinates becomes aware that two of these subordinates are neither friendly nor congenial.
    In making assignments, it would be BEST for the supervisor to
    A. disregard the situation
    B. disregard the situation in making a choice of assignment but emphasize the need for teamwork
    C. investigate the situation to find out who is at fault and give that individual the less desirable assignments until such time as he corrects his attitude
    D. place the unfriendly subordinates in positions where they have as little contact with one another as possible

14._____

15. A DESIRABLE characteristic of a good supervisor is that he should       15._____
    A. identify himself with his subordinates rather than with higher management
    B. inform subordinates of forthcoming changes in policies and programs only when they directly affect the subordinates' activities
    C. make advancement of the subordinates contingent on personal loyalty to the supervisor
    D. make promises to subordinates only when sure of the ability to keep them

16. The supervisor who is MOST likely to be successful is the one who       16._____
    A. refrains from exercising the special privileges of his position
    B. maintains a formal attitude toward his subordinates
    C. maintains an informal attitude toward his subordinates
    D. represents the desires of his subordinate to his superiors

17. Application of sound principles of human relations by a supervisor may be expected to _____ the need for formal discipline.       17._____
    A. decrease          B. have no effect on
    C. increase          D. obviate

18. The MOST important generally approved way to maintain or develop high morale in one's subordinates is to       18._____
    A. give warnings and reprimands in a jocular way
    B. excuse from staff conferences those employees who are busy
    C. keep them informed of new developments and policies of higher management
    D. refrain from criticizing their faults directly

19. In training subordinates, an IMPORTANT principle for the supervisor to recognize is that       19._____
    A. a particular method of instruction will be of substantially equal value for all employees in a given title
    B. it is difficult to train people over 50 years of age because they have little capacity for learning
    C. persons undergoing the same course of training will learn at different rates of speed
    D. training can seldom achieve its purpose unless individual instruction is the chief method used

20. Over an extended period of time, a subordinate is MOST likely to become and remain most productive if the supervisor       20._____
    A. accords praise to the subordinate whenever his work is satisfactory, withholding criticism except in the case of very inferior work
    B. avoids both praise and criticism except for outstandingly good or bad work performed by the subordinate
    C. informs the subordinate of his shortcomings, as viewed by management, while according praise only when highly deserved
    D. keeps the subordinate informed of the degree of satisfaction with which his performance of the job is viewed by management.

## KEY (CORRECT ANSWERS)

| | | | |
|---|---|---|---|
| 1. | C | 11. | D |
| 2. | D | 12. | B |
| 3. | C | 13. | A |
| 4. | A | 14. | D |
| 5. | D | 15. | D |
| 6. | C | 16. | D |
| 7. | A | 17. | A |
| 8. | D | 18. | C |
| 9. | B | 19. | C |
| 10. | D | 20. | D |

# TEST 2

DIRECTIONS: Each question or incomplete statement is followed by several suggested answers or completions. Select the one that BEST answers the question or completes the statement. *PRINT THE LETTER OF THE CORRECT ANSWER IN THE SPACE AT THE RIGHT.*

1. A supervisor has just been told by a subordinate, Mr. Jones, that another employee, Mr. Smith, deliberately disobeyed an important rule of the department by taking home some confidential departmental material.
   Of the following courses of action, it would be MOST advisable for the supervisor FIRST to
   A. discuss the matter privately with both Mr. Jones and Mrs. Smith at the same time
   B. call a meeting of the entire staff and discuss the matter generally without mentioning any employee by name
   C. arrange to supervise Mr. Smith's activities more closely
   D. discuss the matter privately with Mr. Smith

   1.____

2. The one of the following actions which would be MOST efficient and economical for a supervisor to take to minimize the effect of periodical fluctuations in the workload of his unit is to
   A. increase his permanent staff until it is large enough to handle the work of the busy loads
   B. request the purchase of time- and labor-saving equipment to be used primarily during the busy loads
   C. lower, temporarily, the standards for quality of work performance during peak loads
   D. schedule for the slow periods work that is not essential to perform during the busy periods

   2.____

3. Discipline of employees is usually a supervisor's responsibility. There may be several useful forms of disciplinary action.
   Of the following, the form that is LEAST appropriate is the
   A. written reprimand or warning
   B. involuntary transfer to another work setting
   C. demotion or suspension
   D. assignment of added hours of work each week

   3.____

4. Of the following, the MOST effective means of dealing with employee disciplinary problems is to
   A. give personality tests to individuals to identify their psychological problems
   B. distribute and discuss a policy manual containing exact rules governing employee behavior
   C. establish a single, clear penalty to be imposed for all wrongdoing irrespective of degree
   D. have supervisors get to know employees well through social mingling

   4.____

5. A recently developed technique for appraising work performance is to have the supervisor record on a continual basis all significant incidents in each subordinate's behavior that indicate unsuccessful action and those that indicate poor behavior.
Of the following, a MAJOR disadvantage of this method of performance appraisal is that it
   A. often leads to overly close supervision
   B. results in competition among those subordinates being evaluated
   C. tends to result in superficial judgments
   D. lacks objectivity for evaluating performance

5.____

6. Assume that you are a supervisor and have observed the performance of an employee during a period of time. You have concluded that his performance needs improvement.
In order to improve his performance, it would, therefore, be BEST for you to
   A. note your findings in the employee's personnel folder so that his behavior is a matter of record
   B. report the findings to the personnel officer so he can take prompt action
   C. schedule a problem-solving conference with the employee
   D. recommend his transfer to simpler duties

6.____

7. When an employee's absences or latenesses seem to be nearing excessiveness, the supervisor should speak with him to find out what the problem is.
Of the following, if such a discussion produces no reasonable explanation, the discussion usually BEST serves to
   A. affirm clearly the supervisor's adherence to proper policy
   B. alert other employees that such behavior is unacceptable
   C. demonstrate that the supervisor truly represents higher management
   D. notify the employee that his behavior is being observed and evaluated

7.____

8. Assume that an employee willfully and recklessly violates an important agency regulation. The nature of the violation is of such magnitude that it demands immediate action, but the facts of the case are not entirely clear. Further, assume that the supervisor is free to make any of the following recommendations.
The MOST appropriate action for the supervisor to take is to recommend that the employee be
   A. discharged          B. suspended
   C. forced to resign    D. transferred

8.____

9. Although employees' titles may be identical, each position in that title may be considerably different.
Of the following, a supervisor should carefully assign each employee to a specific position based PRIMARILY on the employee's
   A. capability    B. experience    C. education    D. seniority

9.____

10. The one of the following situations where it is MOST appropriate to transfer an employee to a similar assignment is one in which the employee
    A. lacks motivation and interest
    B. experiences a personality conflict with his supervisor
    C. is negligent in the performance of his duties
    D. lacks capacity or ability to perform assigned tasks

10.____

11. The one of the following which is LEAST likely to be affected by improvements in the morale of personnel is employee
    A. skill
    B. absenteeism
    C. turnover
    D. job satisfaction

11.____

12. The one of the following situations in which it is LEAST appropriate for a supervisor to delegate authority to subordinates is where the supervisor
    A. lacks confidence in his own abilities to perform certain work
    B. is overburdened and cannot handle all his responsibilities
    C. refers all disciplinary problems to his subordinate
    D. has to deal with an emergency or crisis

12.____

13. Assume that it has come to your attention that two of your subordinates have shouted at each other and have almost engaged in a fist fight. Luckily, they were separated by some of the other employees.
    Of the following, your BEST immediate course of action would generally be to
    A. reprimand the senior of the two subordinates since he should have known better
    B. hear the story from both employees and any witnesses and then take needed disciplinary action
    C. ignore the matter since nobody was physically hurt
    D. immediately suspend and fine both employees pending a departmental hearing

13.____

14. You have been delegating some of your authority to one of your subordinates because of his leadership potential.
    Which of the following actions is LEAST conducive to the growth and development of this individual for a supervisory position?
    A. Use praise only when it will be effective
    B. Give very detailed instructions and supervise the employee closely to be sure that the instructions ae followed precisely
    C. Let the subordinate proceed with his planned course of action even if mistakes, within a permissible range, are made
    D. Intervene on behalf of the subordinate whenever an assignment becomes difficult for him

14.____

15. A rumor has been spreading in your department concerning the possibility of layoffs due to decreased revenues.
    As a supervisor, you should GENERALLY
    A. deny the rumor, whether it is true or false, in order to keep morale from declining

15.____

B. inform the men to the best of your knowledge about this situation and keep them advised of any new information
C. tell the men to forget about the rumor and concentrate on increasing their productivity
D. ignore the rumor since it is not authorized information

16. Within an organization, every supervisor should know to whom he reports and who reports to him.
The one of the following which is achieved by use of such structured relationships is
    A. unity of command
    B. confidentiality
    C. esprit de corps
    D. promotion opportunities

17. Almost every afternoon, one of your employees comes back from his break ten minutes late without giving you any explanation.
Which of the following actions should you take FIRST in this situation?
    A. Assign the employee to a different type of work and observe whether his behavior changes
    B. Give the employee extra work to do so that he will have to return on time
    C. Ask the employee for an explanation for his lateness
    D. Tell the employee he is jeopardizing the break for everyone

18. When giving instructions to your employees in a group, which one of the following should you make certain to do?
    A. Speak in a casual, off-hand manner
    B. Assume that your employees fully understand the instructions
    C. Write out your instructions beforehand and read them to the employees
    D. Tell exactly who is to do what

19. A fist fight develops between two men under your supervision.
The MOST advisable course of action for you to take FIRST is to
    A. call the police
    B. have the other workers pull them apart
    C. order them to stop
    D. step between the two men

20. You have assigned some difficult and unusual work to one of your most experienced and competent subordinates.
If you notice that he is doing the work incorrectly, you should
    A. assign the work to another employee
    B. reprimand him in private
    C. show him immediately how the work should be done
    D. wait until the job is completed and then correct his errors

## KEY (CORRECT ANSWERS)

| | | | |
|---|---|---|---|
| 1. | D | 11. | A |
| 2. | D | 12. | C |
| 3. | D | 13. | B |
| 4. | B | 14. | B |
| 5. | A | 15. | B |
| 6. | C | 16. | A |
| 7. | D | 17. | C |
| 8. | B | 18. | D |
| 9. | A | 19. | C |
| 10. | B | 20. | C |

# READING COMPREHENSION
# UNDERSTANDING AND INTERPRETING
# WRITTEN MATERIAL

### COMMENTARY

The ability to read and understand written materials—texts, publications, newspapers, orders, directions, expositions—is a skill basic to a functioning democracy and to an efficient business or viable government.

That is why almost all examinations—for beginning, middle, and senior levels—test reading comprehension, directly or indirectly.

The reading test measures how well you understand what you read. This is how it is done: You read a short paragraph and five statements. From the five statements, you choose the one statement, or answer, that is BEST supported by, or best matches, what is said in the paragraph.

---

### SAMPLE QUESTIONS

DIRECTIONS: Each question has five suggested answers, lettered A, B, C, D, and E. Decide which one is the BEST answer. *PRINT THE LETTER OF THE CORRECT ANSWER IN THE SPACE AT THE RIGHT.*

1. The prevention of accidents makes it necessary not only that safety devices be used to guard exposed machinery but also that mechanics be instructed in safety rules which they must follow for their own protection and that the light in the plant be adequate.
   The paragraph BEST supports the statement that industrial accidents
   A. are always avoidable
   B. may be due to ignorance
   C. usually result from inadequate machinery
   D. cannot be entirely overcome
   E. result in damage to machinery

1.____

## ANALYSIS

Remember what you have to do:
- First - Read the paragraph
- Second - Decide what the paragraph means
- Third - Read the five suggested answers.
- Fourth - Select the one answer which BEST matches what the paragraph says or is BEST supported by something in the paragraph. (Sometimes you may have to read the paragraph again in order to be sure which suggested answer is best.

This paragraph is talking about three steps that should be taken to prevent industrial accidents
1. Use safety devices on machines
2. Instruct mechanics in safety rules
3. provide adequate lighting

## SELECTION

With this in mind, let's look at each suggested answer. Each one starts with "Industrial accidents…"

### SUGGESTED ANSWER A
Industrial accidents (A) are always avoidable.
(The paragraph talks about how to avoid accidents, but does not say that accidents are always avoidable.)

### SUGGESTED ANSWER B
Industrial accidents (B) may be due to ignorance.
(One of the steps given in the paragraph to prevent accidents is to instruct mechanics on safety rules. This suggests that lack of knowledge or ignorance of safety rules causes accidents. This suggested answer sounds like a good possibility for being the right answer.)

### SUGGESTED ANSWER C
Industrial accidents (C) usually result from inadequate machinery.
(The paragraph does suggest that exposed machines cause accidents, but it doesn't say that it is the usual cause of accidents. The word usually makes this a wrong answer.)

### SUGGESTED ANSWER D
Industrial accidents (D) cannot be entirely overcome.
(You may know from your own experience that this is a true statement. But that is not what the paragraph is talking about. Therefore, it is NOT the correct answer.)

### SUGGESTED ANSWER E
Industrial accidents (E) result in damage to machinery.
(This is a statement that may or may not be true, but in any case it is NOT covered by the paragraph.)

Looking back, you see that the one suggested answer of the five given that BEST matches what the paragraph says is: Industrial accidents (B) may be due to ignorance.

The CORRECT answer then is B.

Be sure to read ALL the possible answers before you make your choice. You may think that none of the five answers is really good, but choose the BEST one of the five.

---

2. Probably few people realize, as they drive on a concrete road, that steel is used to keep the surface flat in spite of the weight of the busses and trucks. Steel bars, deeply embedded in the concrete, provide sinews to take the stresses so that the stresses cannot crack the slab or make it wavy.
The paragraph BEST supports the statement that a concrete road
   A. is expensive to build
   B. usually cracks under heavy weights
   C. looks like any other road
   D. is used only for heavy traffic
   E. is reinforced with other material

2.____

### ANALYSIS

This paragraph is commenting on the fact that
1. few people realize, as they drive on a concrete road, that steel is deeply embedded
2. steel keeps the surface flat
3. steel bars enable the road to take the stresses without cracking or becoming wavy

### SELECTION

Now read and think about the possible answers:
   A. A concrete road is expensive to build. (Maybe so but that is not what the paragraph is about.)
   B. A concrete road usually cracks under heavy weights. (The paragraph talks about using steel bars to prevent heavy weights from cracking concrete roads. It says nothing about how usual it is for the roads to crack. The word usually makes this suggested answer wrong.)
   C. A concrete road looks like any other road. (This may or may not be true. The important thing to note is that it has nothing to do with what the paragraph is about.)
   D. A concrete road is used only for heavy traffic. (This answer at least has something to do with the paragraph—concrete roads are used with heavy traffic—but it does not say "used only.")
   E. A concrete road is reinforced with other material. (This choice seems to be the correct one on two counts: First, the paragraph does suggest that concrete roads are made

stronger by embedding steel bars in them. This is another way of saying "concrete roads are reinforced with steel bars." Second, by the process of elimination, the other four choices are ruled out as correct answers simply because they do not apply.)

You can be sure that not all the reading questions will be so easy as these.

---

## HINTS FOR ANSWERING READING QUESTIONS

1. Read the paragraph carefully. Then read each suggested answer carefully. Read every word, because often one word can make the difference between a right and a wrong answer.

2. Choose that answer which is supported in the paragraph itself. Do not choose an answer which is a correct statement unless it is based on information in the paragraph.

3. Even though a suggested answer has many of the words used in the paragraph, it may still be wrong.

4. Look out for words—such as *always*, *never*, *entirely*, or *only*—which tend to make a suggested answer wrong.

5. Answer first those questions which you can answer most easily. Then work on the other questions.

6. If you can't figure out the answer to the question, guess.

# READING COMPREHENSION
# UNDERSTANDING WRITTEN MATERIALS
## COMMENTARY

The ability to read and understand written materials—texts, publications, newspapers, orders, directions, expositions—is a skill basic to a functioning democracy and to an efficient business or viable government.

That is why almost all examinations—for beginning, middle, and senior levels—test reading comprehension, directly or indirectly.

The reading test measures how well you understand what you read. This is how it is done: You read a passage followed by several statements. From these statements, you choose the one statement, or answer, that is BEST supported by, or BEST matches, what is said in the paragraph. PRINT THE LETTER OF THE CORRECT ANSWER IN THE SPACE AT THE RIGHT.

### SAMPLE QUESTIONS

DIRECTIONS:   Answer Questions 1 and 2 ONLY according to the information given in the following passage.

1. When a fingerprint technician inks and takes rolled impressions of a subject's fingers, the degree of downward pressure the technician applies is important. The correct pressure may best be determined through experience and observation. It is quite important, however, that the subject be cautioned to relax and not help the fingerprint technician by also applying pressure, as this prevents the fingerprint technician from gaging the amount needed. A method which is helpful in getting the subject to relax his hand is to instruct him to look at some distant object and not to look at his hands.

1. According to this passage, the technician tries to relax the subject's hands by    1.____
    A. instructing him to let his hands hang loosely
    B. telling him that being fingerprinted is painless
    C. asking him to look at this hand instead of some distant object
    D. asking him to look at something other than his hand

2. The subject is asked NOT to press down on his fingers while being fingerprinted    2.____
   because
    A. the impressions taken become rolled
    B. the subject may apply too little downward pressure and spoil the impressions
    C. the technician cannot tell whether he is applying the right degree of pressure
    D. he doesn't have the experience to apply the exact amount of pressure

CORRECT ANSWERS
1. D
2. C

# EXAMINATION SECTION

## TEST 1

DIRECTIONS: Questions 1 through 3 are to be answered on the basis of the following reading passage. *PRINT THE LETTER OF THE CORRECT ANSWER IN THE SPACE AT THE RIGHT.*

Thermostats should be tested in hot water for proper opening. A bucket should be filled with sufficient water to cover the thermostat and fitted with a thermometer suspended in the water so that the sensitive bulb portion does not rest directly on the bucket. The water is then heated on a stove. As the temperature of the water passes the 160-165° range, the thermostat should start to open and should be completely opened when the temperature has risen to 185-190°. Lifting the thermostat into the air should cause a pronounced closing action and the unit should be closed entirely within a short time.

1. The thermostat described above is a device which opens and closes with changes in the
    A. position   B. pressure   C. temperature   D. surroundings

2. According to the above passage, the closing action of the thermostat should be tested by
    A. working the thermostat back and forth
    B. permitting the water to cool gradually
    C. adding cold water to the bucket
    D. removing the thermostat from the bucket

3. The bulb of the thermometer should not rest directly on the bucket because
    A. the bucket gets hotter than the water
    B. the thermometer might be damaged in that position
    C. it is difficult to read the thermometer in that position
    D. the thermometer might interfere with operation of the thermostat

## KEY (CORRECT ANSWERS)

1. C
2. D
3. A

# TEST 2

DIRECTIONS: Questions 1 through 3 are to be answered on the basis of the following reading passage. *PRINT THE LETTER OF THE CORRECT ANSWER IN THE SPACE AT THE RIGHT.*

All idle pumps should be turned daily by hand, and should be run under power at least once a week. Whenever repairs are made on a pump, a record should be kept so that it will be possible to judge the success with which the pump is performing its functions. If a pump fails to deliver liquid, there may be an obstruction in the suction line, the pump's parts may be badly worn, or the packing defective.

1. According to the above passage, pumps  1.____
   A. in use should be turned by hand every day
   B. which are not in use should be run under power every day
   C. which are in daily use should be run under power several times a week
   D. which are not in use should be turned by hand every day

2. According to the above passage, the reason for keeping records of repairs  2.____
   made on pumps is to
   A. make certain that proper maintenance is being performed
   B. discover who is responsible for improper repairs
   C. rate the performance of the pumps
   D. know when to replace worn parts

3. The one of the following causes of pump failure which is NOT mentioned in  3.____
   the above passage is
   A. excessive suction lift       B. clogged lines
   C. bad packing                  D. worn parts

# KEY (CORRECT ANSWERS)

1. A
2. C
3. A

# TEST 3

DIRECTIONS: Questions 1 through 5 are to be answered on the basis of the following reading passage. *PRINT THE LETTER OF THE CORRECT ANSWER IN THE SPACE AT THE RIGHT.*

Floors in warehouses, storerooms, and shipping rooms must be strong enough to stay level under heavy loads. Unevenness of floors may cause boxes of materials to topple and fall. Safe floor load capacities and maximum heights to which boxes may be stacked should be posted conspicuously so all can notice it. Where material in boxes, containers, or cartons of the same weight is regularly stored, it is good practice to paint a horizontal line on the wall indicating the maximum height to which the material may be piled. A qualified expert should determine floor load capacity from the building plans, the age and condition of the floor supports, the type of floor, and other related information.

Working aisles are those from which material is placed into and removed from storage. Working aisles are of two types: transportation aisles, running the length of the building, and cross aisles, running across the width of the building. Deciding on the number, width, and location of working aisles is important. While aisles are necessary and determine boundaries of storage areas, they reduce the space actually used for storage.

1. According to the above passage, how should safe floor load capacities be made known to employees? They should be
   A. given out to each employee
   B. given to supervisors only
   C. printed in large red letters
   D. posted so that they are easily seen

1.____

2. According to the above passage, floor load capacities should be determined by
   A. warehouse supervisors      B. the fire department
   C. qualified experts          D. machine operators

2.____

3. According to the above passage, transportation aisles
   A. run the length of the building
   B. run across the width of the building
   C. are wider than cross aisles
   D. are shorter than cross aisles

3.____

4. According to the above passage, working aisles tend to
   A. take away space that could be used for storage
   B. add to space that could be used for storage
   C. slow down incoming stock
   D. speed up outgoing stock

4.____

5. According to the above passage, unevenness of floors may cause
   A. overall warehouse deterioration    B. piles of stock to fall
   C. materials to spoil                 D. many worker injuries

5.____

2 (#3)

## KEY (CORRECT ANSWERS)

1. D
2. C
3. A
4. A
5. B

# TEST 4

DIRECTIONS: Questions 1 through 3 are to be answered on the basis of the following reading passage. *PRINT THE LETTER OF THE CORRECT ANSWER IN THE SPACE AT THE RIGHT.*

In a retail establishment, any overweight means a distinct loss to the merchant, and even an apparently inconsequential overweight on a single package or sale when multiplied by the total number of transactions, could run into large figures. In addition to the use of reliable scales and weights, and their maintenance in proper condition, there must be proper supervision of the selling force. Such supervision is a difficult matter, particularly on the score of carelessness, as the depositing of extra amounts of material on the scale and failure to remove the same when it overbalances the scale may become a habit. In case of underweight, either in the weighing or by the use of fraudulent scales and weights, the seller soon will hear of it, but there is no reason why the amount weighed out should be in excess of what the customer pays for. Checking sales records against invoices and inventories can supply some indication of the tendency of the sales force to become careless in this field.

1. Of the following, the MOST valid implication of the above passage is that   1.____
   A. all overweights which occur in retail stores are in small amounts
   B. even-arm and uneven-arm balances and weights which are unreliable lead more often to underweights than to overweights
   C. overweights due to errors of salesclerks necessarily lead to large losses by a retailer
   D. supervision to prevent overweights is more important to a retailer than remedial measures after their occurrence

2. Of the following, the MOST valid implication of the above passage is that   2.____
   A. depositing of insufficient amounts of commodities on scales and failure to add to them may become a habit with salesclerks
   B. salesclerks should be trained in understanding and maintenance of scale mechanisms
   C. supervision of salesclerks to prevent careless habits in weighing must depend upon personal observation

3. According to the above passage, the MOST accurate of the following statements is:   3.____
   A. For the most part, the ideas expressed in the passage do not apply to wholesale establishments.
   B. Inventories of commodities prepacked in the store are the only ones which can be used in checking losses due to overweight.
   C. Invoices which give the value and weight of merchandise received are useful in checking losses due to overweights.
   D. The principal value of inventories is to indicate losses due to overweights.

## KEY (CORRECT ANSWERS)

1. D
2. C
3. C

# TEST 5

DIRECTIONS: Questions 1 through 5 are to be answered on the basis of the following reading passage. *PRINT THE LETTER OF THE CORRECT ANSWER IN THE SPACE AT THE RIGHT.*

## TITANIC AIR COMPRESSOR

Valves: The compressors are equipped with Titanic plate valves which are automatic in operation. Valves are so constructed that an entire valve assembly can readily be removed from the head. The valves provide large port areas with short lift and are accurately guided to insure positive seating.

Starting Unloader: Each compressor (or air end) is equipped with a centrifugal governor which is bolted directly to the compressor crank shaft. The governor actuates cylinder relief valves so as to relieve pressure from the cylinders during starting and stopping. The motor is never required to start the compressor tinder load.

Air Strainer: Each cylinder air inlet connection is fitted with a suitable combination air strainer and muffler.

Pistons: Pistons are lightweight castings, ribbed internally to secure strength, and are accurately turned and ground. Each piston is fitted with four (4) rings, two of which are oil control rings. Piston pins are hardened and tempered steel of the full floating type. Bronze bushings are used between piston pin and piston

Connecting Rods: Connecting rods are of solid bronze designed for maximum strength, rigidity, and wear. Crank pins are fitted with renewable steel bushings. Connecting rods are of the one-piece type, there being no bolts, nuts, or cotter pins which can come loose. With this type of construction, wear is reduced to a negligible amount, and adjustment of wrist pin and crank pin bearings is unnecessary.

Main Bearings: Main bearings are of the ball type and are securely held in position by spacers. This type of bearing entirely eliminates the necessity of frequent adjustment or attention. The crank shaft is always in perfect alignment.

Crank Shaft: The crank shaft is a one-piece heat-treated forging of best quality open-hearth steel, of rugged design and of sufficient size to transmit the motor power and any additional stresses which may occur in service. Each crank shaft is counter-balanced (dynamically balanced to reduce vibration to a minimum, and is accurately machined to properly receive the ball-bearing races, crank pin bushing, flexible coupling, and centrifugal governor. Suitable provision is made to insure proper lubrication of all crank shaft bearings and bushings with the minimum amount of attention.

Coupling: Compressor and motor shafts are connected through a Morse Chain Company all-metal enclosed flexible coupling. This coupling consists of two sprockets, one mounted on, and keyed to, each shaft; the sprockets are wrapped by a single Morse Chain, the entire assembly being enclosed in a split aluminum grease-packed cover.

1. The crank pin of the connecting rod is fitted with a renewable bushing made of     1.____
   A. solid bronze                 B. steel
   C. a lightweight casting     D. ball bearings

2.  When the connecting rod is of the one-piece type,
    A. the wrist pins require frequent adjustment
    B. the crank pins require frequent adjustment
    C. the cotter pins frequently will come loose
    D. wear is reduced to a negligible amount

3.  The centrifugal governor is bolted directly to the
    A. compressor crank shaft    B. main bearing
    C. piston pin                D. muffler

4.  The number of oil control rings required for each piston is
    A. one    B. two    C. three    D. four

5.  The compressor and motor shafts are connected through a flexible coupling. These couplings are _____ to the shafts.
    A. keyed    B. brazed    C. soldered    D. press-fit

# KEY (CORRECT ANSWERS)

1. B
2. D
3. A
4. B
5. A

# TEST 6

DIRECTIONS: Questions 1 through 6 are to be answered on the basis of the following reading passage. *PRINT THE LETTER OF THE CORRECT ANSWER IN THE SPACE AT THE RIGHT.*

Perhaps the strongest argument the mass transit backer has is the advantage in efficiency that mass transit has over the automobile in the urban traffic picture. It has been estimated that given comparable location and construction conditions, the subway can carry four times as many passengers per hour and cost half as much to build as urban highways. Yet public apathy regarding the mass transportation movement in the 1960's resulted in the building of more roads. Planned to provide 42,000 miles of highways in the period from 1956-72, including 7,500 miles within cities, the Federal Highway System project is now about two-thirds completed. The Highway Trust Fund supplies 90 percent of the cost of the system, with state and local sources putting up the rest of the money. By contrast, a municipality as had to put up the bulk of the cost of a rapid transit system. Although the system and its Trust Fund have come under attack in the past few years from environmentalists and groups opposed to the continued building of urban freeways—considered to be the most expensive, destructive, and inefficient segments of the system—a move by them to get the Trust Fund transformed into a general transportation fund at the expiration of the present program in 1972 seems to be headed nowhere.

1. Given similar building conditions and locations, a city that builds a subway instead of a highway can expect to receive for each dollar spent _____ as much transport value.
   A. half        B. twice        C. four times        D. eight times        1._____

2. The general attitude of the public in the past ten years toward the mass transportation movement has been
   A. favorable        B. indifferent        C. enthusiastic        D. unfriendly        2._____

3. The number of miles of highways still to be completed in the Federal Highway System project is MOST NEARLY
   A. 2,500        B. 5,000        C. 14,000        D. 28,000        3._____

4. What do certain groups who object to some features of the Federal Highway System program want to do with the Highway Trust Fund after 1972?        4._____
   A. Extend it in order to complete the project
   B. Change it so that the money can be used for all types of transportation
   C. End it even if the project is not completed
   D. Change it so that the money will be used only for urban freeways

5. Which one of the following statements is a VALID conclusion based on the facts in the above passage?        5._____
   A. The advantage of greater efficiency is the only argument that supporters of the mass transportation movement can offer.
   B. It was easier for cities to build roads rather than mass transit systems in the last 15 years because of the large financial contribution made by the Federal Government.

2 (#6)

- C. Mass transit systems cause as much congestion and air pollution in cities as automobiles.
- D. In 1972, the Highway Trust Fund becomes a general transportation fund.

6. The MAIN idea or theme of the above passage is that the    6.____
   - A. cost of the Federal Highway System is shared by the federal, state, and local governments
   - B. public is against spending money for building mass transportation facilities in the cities
   - C. cities would benefit more from expansion and improvement of their mass transit systems than from the building of more highways
   - D. building of mass transportation facilities has been slowed by the Highway Trust Fund

## KEY (CORRECT ANSWERS)

1. D
2. B
3. C
4. B
5. B
6. C

# TEST 7

DIRECTIONS: Questions 1 through 5 are to be answered on the basis of the following reading passage. *PRINT THE LETTER OF THE CORRECT ANSWER IN THE SPACE AT THE RIGHT.*

The use of role-playing as a training technique was developed during the past decade by social scientists, particularly psychologists, who have been active in training experiments. Originally, this technique was applied by clinical psychologists who discovered that a patient appears to gain understanding of an emotionally disturbing situation when encouraged to act out roles in that situation. As applied in government and business organizations, the purpose of role-playing is to aid employees to understand certain work problems involving interpersonal relations and to enable observers to evaluate various reactions to them. Thus, for example, on the problem of handling grievances, two individuals from the group might be selected to act out extemporaneously the parts of subordinate and supervisor. When this situation is enacted by various pairs among the class and the techniques and results are discussed, the members of the group are presumed to reach conclusions about the most effective means of handling similar situations. Often the use or role reversal, where participants take parts different from their actual work roles, assists individuals to gain more insight into other people's problems and viewpoints. Although role-playing can be a rewarding training device, the trainer must be aware of his responsibilities. If this technique is to be successful, thorough briefing of both actors and observers as to the situation in question, the participants' roles, and what to look for, is essential.

1. The role-playing technique was FIRST used for the purpose of
   A. measuring the effectiveness of training programs
   B. training supervisors in business organizations
   C. treating emotionally disturbed patients
   D. handling employee grievances

2. When role-playing is used in private business as a training device, the CHIEF aim is to
   A. develop better relations between supervisor and subordinate in the handling of grievances
   B. come up with a solution to a specific problem that has arisen
   C. determine the training needs of the group
   D. increase employee understanding of the human-relation factors in work situations

3. From the above passage, it is MOST reasonable to conclude that when role-playing is used, it is preferable to have the roles acted out by
   A. only one set of actors
   B. no more than two sets of actors
   C. several different sets of actors
   D. the trainer or trainers of the group

4. It can be inferred from the above passage that a limitation of role-playing as a training method is that
    A. many work situations do not lend themselves to role-play
    B. employees are not experienced enough as actors to play the roles realistically
    C. only trainers who have psychological training can use it successfully
    D. participants who are observing and not acting do not benefit from it

5. To obtain *good* results from the use of role-play in training, a trainer should give participants
    A. a minimum of information about the situation so that they can act spontaneously
    B. scripts which illustrate the best method for handling the situation
    C. a complete explanation of the problem and the roles to be acted out
    D. a summary of work problems which involve interpersonal relations

## KEY (CORRECT ANSWERS)

1. C
2. D
3. C
4. A
5. C

# EDUCATING AND INTERACTING WITH THE PUBLIC

These questions test for knowledge of techniques used to interact effectively with individual citizens and/or community groups, to educate or inform them about topics of concern, to publicize or clarify agency programs or policies, to negotiate conflicts or resolve complaints, and to represent one's agency or program in a manner in keeping with good public relations practices. Questions may also cover interacting with others in cooperative efforts of public outreach or service. There will be 15 questions in this subject area on the written test.

TEST TASK:
You will be presented with a variety of situations in which you must apply knowledge of how best to interact with other people.

SAMPLE QUESTION:
A person approaches you expressing anger about a recent action by your department. Which one of the following should be your first response to this person?

    A. Interrupt to say you cannot discuss the situation until he calms down.
    B. Say you are sorry that he has been negatively affected by your department's action.
    C. Listen and express understanding that he has been upset by your department's action.
    D. Give him an explanation of the reasons for your department's action.

The correct answer to this sample question is choice C

C. SOLUTION:

**Choice A** *is not correct.* It would be inappropriate to interrupt. In addition, saying that you cannot discuss the situation until the person calms down will likely aggravate him further.

**Choice B** *is not correct.* Apologizing for your department's action implies that the action was improper.

**Choice C is the correct answer to this question.** By listening and expressing understanding that your department's action has upset him, you demonstrate that you have heard and understand his feelings and point of view.

**Choice D** *is not correct.* While an explanation of the reasons for the action may be appropriate at a later time, at this moment the person is angry and would not be receptive to such an explanation.

# EXAMINATION SECTION
# TEST 1

DIRECTIONS: Each question or incomplete statement is followed by several suggested answers or completions. Select the one that BEST answers the question or completes the statement. *PRINT THE LETTER OF THE CORRECT ANSWER IN THE SPACE AT THE RIGHT.*

1. A group member who starts out at the same level as other group members and is able to move into a leadership position within that group would be described as what kind of a leader? 1.____
   A. Autocratic    B. Democratic    C. Emergent    D. Informal

2. Your boss is only effective as the leader of your department when you and your coworkers are motivated experts on the topic at hand. If any of you do not really have expertise in a given field, his leadership falters somewhat. What type of leader is your boss? 2.____
   A. Laissez-faire    B. Technical    C. Democratic    D. Autocratic

3. If a leader is in charge of an inexperienced group that does not have the appropriate information and proficiency to successfully complete a task, which of the following approaches should the leader use in order for success to follow within the group? 3.____
   A. Yelling    B. Delegating    C. Participating    D. Selling

4. If you are a democratic leader, which of the following styles will be reflective of your leadership technique? 4.____
   A. Participating    B. Telling    C. Yelling    D. Delegating

5. In producing equality in group member participation, which of the following should a leader NOT do? 5.____
   A. Make a statement or ask a question after each person in the group has said something
   B. Avoid taking a position during disagreements
   C. Limit comments to specific individuals within the group
   D. Control dominating speakers

6. Social capital is BEST defined as 6.____
   A. social connections that help us make more money
   B. social connections that improve our lives
   C. a type of connection that experts believe is becoming more common in Europe than the United States.
   D. none of the above

7. Communication is not simply sending a message. It is creating true 7.____
   A. connectivity              B. understanding
   C. empathy                   D. power

8. Of the following, which is NOT a part of the speech communication process?
   A. Feedback
   B. Central idea
   C. Interference
   D. Ethics

9. You are leading a meeting and afterwards your colleagues tell you they didn't quite understand what you were communicating verbally and nonverbally to them. Which part of the communication process do you need to work on?
   A. Channel
   B. Main idea
   C. Message
   D. Specific purpose

10. If nonverbal messages contradict verbal symbols, you are sending what kind of message to your public?
    A. Clear
    B. Mixed
    C. Controversial
    D. Negative

11. Which of the following would a public speaker use to deliver verbal symbols?
    A. Words
    B. Gestures
    C. Tone
    D. Facial expression

12. You are in the process of taking a course on interacting with the public. Your instructor starts talking about "the pathway" used to transmit a message. He explains that "the pathway" is better known as a
    A. link
    B. loop
    C. transmitter
    D. channel

13. You finish an informational meeting with members of a community concerning a new park that will be built nearby. Afterwards, you are seeking feedback from them. Which of the following would NOT be a form of helpful feedback to you?
    A. Listeners raise their hands to point out a mistake
    B. Videotape the presentation
    C. Have colleagues and/or friends critique your presentation
    D. Hand out evaluation forms to listeners and have them fill it out after the presentation

14. Many public speaking experts have often repeated the famous quote, "A yawn is a silent _____," which references the quality of engagement within a presentation.
    A. rudeness
    B. insult
    C. shout
    D. protest

15. If a child is running around during your speech and making a lot of noise, what type of interference would that be?
    A. Situational
    B. External
    C. Internal
    D. Intentional

16. According to multiple recent surveys, of the five biggest mistakes that speakers make during a presentation, which one is the WORST?
    A. Being poorly prepared
    B. Trying to cover too much in one speech
    C. Failing to tailor a speech to the needs and interests of the audience
    D. Being boring

17. One of your colleagues has been asked to lead a meeting, and she confides in you that she suffers from excessive stage fright. Which of the following areas should you advise her to focus on to prevent her fear?
    A. Preparation
    B. Self-confidence
    C. Experience
    D. Sense of humor

17.____

18. When interacting with the public, which of the following elements should you NEVER imagine before engaging in public speaking?
    A. Effective delivery
    B. Nervousness
    C. Possibility of failure
    D. Success

18.____

19. A spokesperson is giving a speech to community members and you are evaluating him. You notice he tends to focus too much on himself and not enough on his audience. What is one piece of advice you can give him so he can shift his focus more to his audience?
    A. Change his amount of eye contact
    B. Work on facial expressions
    C. Alter his style of speaking
    D. All of the above

19.____

20. Most experts agree that the best way to eliminate excess energy would be to do all of the following EXCEPT
    A. using visual aids
    B. gripping the lectern
    C. walking to the right and left occasionally
    D. making gestures

20.____

21. A woman has lived in Newville her whole life. Recently, the Newville public works department made a policy change that angered her since it completely rearranged her schedule. She calls you on the phone and displays her displeasure with your department's recent policy change. What is the FIRST response you should have toward her?
    A. Interrupt her to say you cannot discuss the situation until she calms down
    B. Apologize to her that she has been negatively affected by the public works department
    C. Listen to her and demonstrate comprehension of her situation and why she was upset by your department's action
    D. Give her a detailed explanation of the reasons for the policy change

21.____

22. Which of the following is generally TRUE regarding public opinion?
    A. It is hard to move people toward a strong opinion on anything
    B. It is easy to move people toward a strong opinion on anything
    C. Most public relations are devoted to repairing negative public opinion about individuals
    D. It is easier than previously thought to move people away from an opinion they hold

22.____

23. Influencing a community member's attitude really comes down to which of the following?
    A. Journalism
    B. Public relations
    C. Social psychology
    D. Social action groups

23.____

24. If you attend a town hall meeting in which community members will bring up issues that require you to explain why your organization made the decisions it made, you will need to persuade them using evidence that is virtually indisputable. Which type of evidence should you stick to when explaining answers to the public?
    A. Facts
    B. Personal experience
    C. Emotions
    D. Using what appeals to the target public

25. In the last decade, especially after all the organizational and governmental scandals, public institutions must do which of the following in order to be successful?
    A. Work hard to earn and sustain favorable public opinion
    B. Trust the instincts expressed by the general public
    C. Be cognizant of the media's power
    D. Place the needs of the executives ahead of the needs of the public and other constituents

## KEY (CORRECT ANSWERS)

| | | | |
|---|---|---|---|
| 1. | C | 11. | A |
| 2. | A | 12. | D |
| 3. | B | 13. | A |
| 4. | D | 14. | C |
| 5. | A | 15. | B |
| 6. | B | 16. | C |
| 7. | B | 17. | A |
| 8. | D | 18. | B |
| 9. | C | 19. | D |
| 10. | B | 20. | B |

21. C
22. D
23. B
24. A
25. A

# TEST 2

DIRECTIONS: Each question or incomplete statement is followed by several suggested answers or completions. Select the one that BEST answers the question or completes the statement. *PRINT THE LETTER OF THE CORRECT ANSWER IN THE SPACE AT THE RIGHT.*

1. Unique attributes of the Internet that people can enjoy include all of the following EXCEPT  1.____
   A. immediacy
   B. low cost
   C. pervasiveness
   D. value for building one-to-one human relationships

2. Which of the following is a reason that social media can be more effective than traditional means of advertising and communication?  2.____
   A. When someone mentions your brand in social media, there is much more potential for other people to notice
   B. It is easier to decipher tone and purpose through Twitter or Facebook than through personal communication
   C. Most of the people who would be interested in your brand or service are comfortable and familiar with using social media
   D. Almost anyone can step into a media relations role if primarily using social media, because it is easy to communicate effectively through social media platforms

3. You are tasked with building publicity for the upcoming reveal of a new art installation in the town you work in. Your boss tells you to contact journalists, reporters and bloggers to help spread the word. Which of the following would be the MOST effective way of getting the media to help build coverage?  3.____
   A. Send out a mass e-mail to any media members in the area detailing the art installation and why you need coverage for it
   B. Call each media outlet and find out who would most likely cover and build publicity for your project. Then reach out to them either face-to-face or through a phone call
   C. Using Twitter, tweet at the media members and introduce yourself and your art installation and ask them to help spread the word
   D. None of the above

4. When using written communication, which of the following is a MAJOR challenge of writing to listeners?  4.____
   A. Providing lots of statistics
   B. Grabbing the attention of the listener quickly
   C. Providing information that is easily reviewed
   D. Presenting lots of incidentals

5. In order to communicate well in writing, which of the following pieces of advice sounds good but doesn't actually help you?
   A. Write material for all audiences rather than focusing on one
   B. Think before writing
   C. Write simply and with clarity
   D. Write and rewrite until you have a polished, finished product

6. You send out a public newsletter that details a project that your team is currently working on. One week later, an employee on your team tells you she has received multiple phone calls from confused constituents claiming that the newsletter's readability was low. When you send out a corrected newsletter, you need to make sure that your communication is easy to
   A. read   B. hear   C. edit   D. comprehend

7. You work for a biomedical company as a public outreach advocate. One day, an exciting e-mail circulates internally that states one of your scientists has discovered a cure for leukemia and your supervisor tasks you with writing the release. When writing the release, the newsworthy element inherent in the story is
   A. oddity   B. conflict   C. impact   D. proximity

8. When communicating with the public through the Internet, news releases
   A. should not be sent via e-mail
   B. should be succinct
   C. should be sent via "snail mail"
   D. none of the above

9. What is the MAJOR advantage of organizational publications? Their ability to
   A. give sponsoring organizations a means of uncontrolled communications
   B. deliver specific, detailed information to narrowly defined target publics
   C. avoid the problems typically associated with two-way media
   D. provide a revenue source for sponsoring organizations

10. You are confronted by a question from a reporter that you do not know the answer to. What should you do?
    A. Give them other information you are certain is right
    B. Tell them that information is "off the record" and will be distributed later
    C. Say "no comment" rather than look like you're uninformed
    D. Admit that you don't know but promise to provide the information later

11. Often times, an organization will run situation analysis before they share information with the public. Which one of these "internal factors" is usually associated with a situational analysis?
    A. A communication audit
    B. Community focus groups
    C. A list of media contacts
    D. Strategy suggestions

3 (#2)

12. When you are hired, your first task is to start a process of identifying who are involved and affected by a situation central to your organization. This process is MOST commonly referred to as a(n)
    A. situation interview
    B. communication audit
    C. exploratory survey
    D. stakeholder analysis

12.____

13. Once a public outreach plan is in the summative evaluation phase, which of the following is generally associated with it?
    A. Impact
    B. Implementation
    C. Attitude change
    D. Preparation

13.____

14. Which of the following Internet-related challenges is MOST significant in the public relations field?
    A. Finding stable, cost-effective internet provides
    B. Representing clients using new social media environments
    C. Staying abreast of changing technology
    D. Training staff to use social media

14.____

15. Which of the following BEST defines a public issue? Any
    A. problem that brings a public lawsuit
    B. concern that is of mutual distress to competitors
    C. issue that is of mutual concern to an organization and its stakeholders
    D. problem that is not a concern to an organization and/or one of its stakeholders

15.____

16. A handful of people are posting misleading and/or negative information about your organization. What is the MOST proactive approach to handling this situation?
    A. Buy up enough shares in the site where the negative posts are, and prevent those users from posting again
    B. Post anonymous comments on the sites to help combat the negativity
    C. Prepare news releases that discredit the inaccuracies
    D. Make policy changes to address complaints highlighted on the sites

16.____

17. Your supervisor has recently asked you to review present and future realities for interacting with the public. Why is it important to continually review these?
    A. It helps develop your vision statement
    B. It helps interpret trends for management
    C. It helps construe the organization's business plan
    D. To know what path the company should pursue

17.____

18. You are the community relations director for the public water utility plant that has been the focus of a group of activists who are opposed to the addition of fluoride to drinking water. These objectors are not only at the plant each day, but they are also very active on social media inciting negativity towards the practice. As the director of the plant, you have overwhelming evidence that contradicts what the protestors are arguing. You want to combat their social media with your own internet plan. Which of the following is the MOST appropriate action for you to take?

   A. Use utility employees to write the blog, posing as healthcare professionals
   B. Reach out to medical professionals to volunteer to tweet and message community members under their own identities, but with no reference to the utility company
   C. Write a blog yourself, identifying yourself as an employee, and quote the scientific opinions of a variety of sources
   D. Pay for medical professionals to respond through the internet, identifying the utility as their sponsor, but without disclosing the compensation

18.____

19. You have recently completed an advertising campaign to help assuage the anger of the community at changes in the upcoming summer program for the city. Which of the following measurements would be MOST effective for evaluating the campaign's impact on audience attitude?

   A. A content analysis of media coverage
   B. Studying blog postings about the issue
   C. Analyzing pre- and post-numbers of people signed up for the summer programs
   D. Conducting a pre- and post-analysis of public opinions

19.____

20. In order to measure how policy changes will affect the public, you recommend that your supervisors first run a focus group for research. They like the idea, but want you to be in charge of running the group. Which of the following should you keep in mind as you form the focus group?

   A. Participants need to be randomly selected
   B. Make sure participants are radically different from one another so you get a range of opinions
   C. Include at least seven or more people in the group. Otherwise, the sample is too small to draw any conclusions.
   D. Formulate a research plan and use it as a script so you can make sure the results are ones that will work for you and your supervisors

20.____

21. The public university has recently come under fire for not offering enough tuition savings options for students. You have been hired to help promote the programs they offer including new savings programs. What is the MOST appropriate first step for you to take?

   A. Research pricing and development costs for the services
   B. Develop a survey to discover which factors impact families' savings
   C. Conduct a situation analysis to gain better understanding of the issues
   D. Hold a focus group to determine which messages would be most effective for your program

21.____

5 (#2)

22. After receiving feedback from the public on a new program, you are concerned the results have been tainted by courtesy bias. You plan on sending out a new questionnaire, but you need to make sure the bias is discouraged in it. Which of the following techniques will be MOST effective at decreasing the partiality?
    A. Make questionnaire responses confidential
    B. Employ an outside firm to run the survey
    C. Offer a larger range of responses in the survey
    D. Both "A" and "C"

22._____

23. You have just relocated from Omaha, Nebraska to a branch in Chicago, Illinois. In order to communicate well while in Chicago, you must remember that
    A. most publics have the same needs
    B. all publics are most interested only in technology you are using
    C. each audience has its own special needs and require different types of communication
    D. all audiences' needs overlap

23._____

24. Recently, the Parks and Recreation Department has come under fire because it has been accused of too much marketing and not enough public relations. Which of the following, if true, would lend credibility to these accusations?
    A. Employees are focused on signing citizens up for as many different camps and activities available over the summer as possible
    B. Management consistently tries to send appreciation gifts to members of the community when they have volunteered or attending an activity sponsored by the Park district
    C. Weekly meetings are held to determine how to best improve the Park district's image as it relates to consumers
    D. Parks and Recreation is primarily focused on making sure the public enjoys their activities and trusts them to put on educational programs for the children

24._____

25. During your speech, a community member stands up and accuses you of "spinning" a story. Which of the following BEST describes their accusation?
    A. You are relating a message through an agreed-upon ethical practice within the public relations community
    B. You are twisting a message to create performance where there is none
    C. You are trying to preserve hard-earned credibility
    D. You are providing the media with balanced and accurate information

25._____

## KEY (CORRECT ANSWERS)

| | | | |
|---|---|---|---|
| 1. | D | 11. | A |
| 2. | A | 12. | D |
| 3. | C | 13. | A |
| 4. | B | 14. | C |
| 5. | D | 15. | C |
| | | | |
| 6. | D | 16. | B |
| 7. | C | 17. | A |
| 8. | B | 18. | C |
| 9. | B | 19. | D |
| 10. | D | 20. | A |

21. C
22. D
23. C
24. A
25. B

# TEST 3

DIRECTIONS: Each question or incomplete statement is followed by several suggested answers or completions. Select the one that BEST answers the question or completes the statement. *PRINT THE LETTER OF THE CORRECT ANSWER IN THE SPACE AT THE RIGHT.*

1. In order to be successful in relating to the public, all of the following are vital EXCEPT
   A. performance
   B. relationship building
   C. formal education
   D. diversity of experience

    1.____

2. Which of the following is TRUE of communicating well regarding public relations experts?
   A. It will differentiate you and your role from others with special skills in the organization you work for
   B. It should be handled delicately in order to avoid upsetting stakeholders
   C. It is not as important as looking fashionable
   D. It is less important than understanding bureaucratic peculiarities

    2.____

3. You are critiquing a staffer who will lead an important meeting in two days and you note that she keeps using words that are steeped with connotation. You tell her to be careful of these words. Why?
   A. They transmit meaning too clearly, and you always want to leave wiggle room in your meaning
   B. They transmit the dictionary definition of a word that makes for a boring presentation
   C. They transmit meaning with an emotional overtone that could lead to misunderstanding in an overall message
   D. They lend themselves to stereotyping

    3.____

4. If you are trying to avoid biasing your intended audience, which of the following factors could help with that?
   A. Symbols
   B. Objective reporting by media
   C. Semantics
   D. Peers

    4.____

5. Of the following, which trait is MOST desirable when working with the public?
   A. Having the "gift for gab"
   B. Being an elite strategist
   C. Being able to leap organizational boundaries
   D. Performing well, especially in crises

    5.____

6. Which of the following areas is likely to see continual growth in the practice of public relations?
   A. Healthcare
   B. Social media
   C. Law enforcement
   D. None of the above

    6.____

7. What is the MOST commonly used public relations tactic?
   A. A news release
   B. A special event
   C. A PSA (public service announcement)
   D. A full feature news article

7.____

8. You have just been assigned to help with a new advertising campaign that will promote the new services offered by your organization. One major component of the new campaign will focus on publicity through photographs. Knowing you need to get this part of the project right, which of the following is the BEST tip to remember when taking PR photos?
   A. Don't use action shots because they usually wind up blurry
   B. Make sure there is good contrast and sharp detail
   C. Ensure that the product/services are the biggest thing(s) in the photo
   D. Photograph multiple people rather than only one

8.____

9. Which of the following situations would merit holding a press conference?
   A. When a corporation is restructured
   B. When a new public relations employee has been hired
   C. When information is of minor relevance to a specific audience
   D. When there is a new product to be released

9.____

10. On average, how long should an announcement to the public last on the radio?
    A. 2 minutes    B. 20 seconds    C. 1 minute    D. 10 seconds

10.____

11. In educating the public, you need to develop a PR plan and analyze each situation that could arise. Which of the following should NOT be a part of the analysis?
    A. Research                       B. Message crafting
    C. Creating a problem statement   D. Asking the 5 W's and the H

11.____

12. You are in charge of promoting an event in the near future, but social media is unavailable to you at this time. Which of the following is the BEST way to get your message out to the media and, therefore, the public?
    A. An Op-Ed piece in the local newspaper
    B. A press conference
    C. A newsletter
    D. A news release

12.____

13. In the past few months, you and your colleagues have been accused of "doublespeak". Which of the following excerpts from presentations you have used could you defend and explain why it would NOT be an example of "doublespeak"?
    A. You called combat "fighting"
    B. Fred referred to genocide as "ethnic cleansing"
    C. Your boss referred to recent layoffs as "downsizing"
    D. Susie called the janitor a "custodial engineer"

13.____

14. In relating to the public, which of the following reflects key words in defining modern day PR?
    A. Deliberate, public interest, management function
    B. Persuasive, manipulative, improvisation
    C. Management, technical, flexible
    D. Influential, creative, evaluative

15. How is educating and relating to the public different from being a journalist, marketing agent, or advertiser?
    A. It is more focused on advocacy
    B. It is about getting "free" press coverage
    C. It is about building relationships with various demographics
    D. All of the above

16. Of the following, what is the BEST tactic for learning employee attitudes?
    A. Internal communications audit
    B. Research
    C. Conference meeting
    D. Both A and B

17. When releasing news to the public, you should make sure it reads at a _____-grade reading level.
    A. 5th    B. 12th    C. 9th    D. 7th

18. If you are using a euphemism that actually changes the meaning/impact of a concept you are trying to relay, what is that called?
    A. Insider language
    B. Doublespeak
    C. Stylizing
    D. Plagiarism

19. Which of the following should be included in a public relations campaign if you want to ensure people will hear, understand, and believe your message?
    A. Repetition
    B. Imagery
    C. Thoroughness
    D. Acceptance

20. In PR, what is it called when you track coverage and compare it over a period of time?
    A. Bookmarking
    B. Benchmarking
    C. Comparison analysis
    D. Correspondence

21. What is a baseline study PRIMARILY used for?
    A. To determine changes in audience perception and attitude
    B. To figure out how well your company is doing in the marketplace compared to your competitors
    C. To find out the cost of buying space taken up by a particular article if that article is an advertisement
    D. None of the above

22. Of the following people, who would BEST be considered a modern role model for successful public relations?
    A. Phineas T. Barnum (Barnum and Bailey)
    B. Ivy Lee
    C. Andrew Jackson
    D. Sir Walter Raleigh

23. If your organization has recently participated in a "publicity stunt," what type of PR strategy have you just used?
    A. Community
    B. Lobbying
    C. News management
    D. Crisis management

24. You tell your supervisor that you want to start using video press releases. When he presses you to explain why, you tell him that you want to take advantage of the fact that
    A. many news agencies don't review them ahead of broadcasting
    B. most reporters hired to create them have contacts within the industry
    C. they cover stories that some local news organizations cannot
    D. the production value may be better than those at local stations

25. A _____ is a type of news leak in which the source reveals large policy changes are on the table.
    A. disclosure    B. hook    C. exclusive    D. trial balloon

## KEY (CORRECT ANSWERS)

| | | | | |
|---|---|---|---|---|
| 1. | C | | 11. | B |
| 2. | B | | 12. | D |
| 3. | C | | 13. | A |
| 4. | B | | 14. | A |
| 5. | D | | 15. | D |
| | | | | |
| 6. | B | | 16. | D |
| 7. | A | | 17. | C |
| 8. | B | | 18. | B |
| 9. | D | | 19. | A |
| 10. | C | | 20. | B |

21. A
22. B
23. C
24. C
25. D

# TEST 4

DIRECTIONS: Each question or incomplete statement is followed by several suggested answers or completions. Select the one that BEST answers the question or completes the statement. *PRINT THE LETTER OF THE CORRECT ANSWER IN THE SPACE AT THE RIGHT.*

1. The Facial Feedback Hypothesis is a popular nonverbal theory that is BEST defined as
    A. people mirroring each other's facial expressions
    B. emotions leading to certain facial expressions
    C. facial expression can lead to the experience of certain emotions
    D. looking into a mirror while making a facial expression can cause one to change their facial expression

    1.____

2. Of the following, which is NOT recognized as a function of smiling?
    A. It provides feedback.
    B. It signals disinterest.
    C. It helps establish rapport.
    D. It signals attentiveness.

    2.____

3. When facial expressions are limited by cultural expectations, that is referred to as
    A. display rules
    B. syntactic displays
    C. adaptors
    D. interaction intensification

    3.____

4. Of the following, which is recognized as part of the six basic emotions across cultures globally?
    A. Guilt
    B. Happiness
    C. Fear
    D. Both B and C

    4.____

5. Which kinds of communication scenarios are more likely to see leadership roles develop from?
    A. Small group
    B. Intrapersonal communication
    C. Face-to-face public communication
    D. Text messaging

    5.____

6. Which of the following highlights the key difference between small group communication and organizational communication?
    A. Feedback is easier and more immediate in organizational.
    B. Communication is more informal in small group communication.
    C. The message is easier to adapt to the specific needs of the receiver in organizational communication.
    D. People are more spread out in small group communication.

    6.____

7. Which of the following would be an example of mediated communication?
    A. A principal addresses the student body in a speech.
    B. Two friends communicate while they work together in class.
    C. An employee texts his coworkers to see if they want to hang out after work.
    D. Three friends joke with one another while attending a concert.

    7.____

8. Which of the following is FALSE concerning the way interpersonal relationships can affect us physically?
    A. Without interpersonal relationships, we can become sick
    B. These interpersonal relationships are necessary for humans; according to most research, humans raised in isolation are less healthy than those raised with others
    C. Humans are not the only mammals that need relationships in order to survive and thrive
    D. Interpersonal relationships are necessary until about age 12, but not later in adulthood

9. Which of the following is a characteristic of public relationships as they compare to private relationships?
    A. Intrinsic rewards
    B. Normative rules
    C. Use of particularistic knowledge
    D. Small number of intimates

10. When someone asks how you know they were angry, it is likely they fall into which style of facial expressions?
    A. Withholder
    B. Revealer
    C. Frozen-affect expressor
    D. Unwitting expressor

11. The theory of expectancy violations is BEST defined as
    A. nonverbal behavior reciprocated based primarily on positive or negative valence and the perceived reward value of the other person
    B. the process of intimacy exchange within a dyad relationship
    C. a social rule that says we should repay in kind what another has provided us
    D. none of the above

12. If an employee has a very good idea of what is and is not socially acceptable in any given situation, which kind of linguistic competence is she strong in?
    A. Phonemic    B. Syntactic    C. Pragmatic    D. Semantic

13. Which of the following would NOT be considered sexist language?
    A. Although a girl, Sonia is very brave.
    B. A gorgeous model, Johnny also likes to use his surfboard on the weekends.
    C. Jimmy's brother is a male nurse.
    D. None; all are considered to be sexist.

14. What is it called when individual experience, and NOT conventional agreement, creates meaning?
    A. Small talk communication
    B. Denotative meaning
    C. Connotative meaning
    D. Self-reflexive communication

15. Which of the following kinds of communication do students spend the MOST time engaged in?
    A. Listening    B. Writing    C. Reading    D. Speaking

16. Which of the following would be evidence of active listening?　　　　　　　　　　16._____
    A. Maintain eye contact　　　　　B. Nodding and making eye contact
    C. Asking for clarification　　　　D. All of the above

17. When listening in an evaluative context, which of the following must be done　　17._____
    for it to be considered successful?
    A. Precisely disseminate stimuli in a message
    B. Comprehend the intended meaning of a message
    C. Make critical assessments of the accuracy of the facts in a message
    D. All of the above

18. A friend visits one day and tells you she thinks her husband is cheating on her　18._____
    with his ex-wife. She tells you she doesn't know what to do because she can't
    imagine living without him. If you wanted to paraphrase, which of the following
    BEST exemplifies that?
    A. "You are feeling insecure because you don't have a very good
       relationship with your husband."
    B. "You're afraid your husband is seeing his ex-wife behind your back; you
       don't know what to do; and you can't live without him."
    C. "You're afraid that your husband may still have feelings for his ex-wife and
       you're afraid you'll lose him."
    D. "Don't worry; his ex-wife is not back with him. You're just being paranoid."

19. When we form impressions of others, when might the recency effect impact　　19._____
    our assessments? If we
    A. focus on our own feelings instead of the feelings of others
    B. are motivated to be more accurate or expect to be held accountable for
       our own perceptions
    C. engage in self-monitoring of our behaviors
    D. employ the discounting rule

20. Which of the following BEST defines a "modal self"?　　　　　　　　　　　　　　20._____
    A. The ideal person for a social order
    B. A person who does not go to extremes
    C. The kind of self valued in the 20$^{th}$ century but not the 21$^{st}$ century
    D. The person who monitors his own behavior in social situations

21. Which of the following is TRUE of today's society?　　　　　　　　　　　　　　　21._____
    A. People are less selfish than they have ever been.
    B. People spend most of their time trying to be a single, unitary self.
    C. People have many short-lived relationships leading to their notions of
       themselves changing easily.
    D. People try to be frugal, honorable, and self-sacrificing.

22. A man's childhood consisted of a dismissing attachment style. Which of the following behaviors will he MOST likely exhibit as an adult?
    A. Anxiousness and ambivalence
    B. Obsessive friendliness and dependence
    C. Autonomy and distance from others
    D. Rhetorical sensitivity

23. When practicing self-disclosure, which of the following is a good rule of thumb?
    A. Be sure to disclose more than your partner
    B. Reserve your most important disclosures for people you know well
    C. Ignore the style of disclosure; the only thing that is important is content
    D. All of the above

24. During your first meeting as project leader, you approach your group and inform them that John will serve as your assistant project leader. He will be responsible for chairing team meetings and establishing the agenda. When John is given this formal leadership position, what type of power does he have over the other members of the project?
    A. Legitimate    B. Reward    C. Expert    D. Punishment

25. If you bring an employee to lead a project because she is knowledgeable and skilled in the area the project focuses on, what type of power does she possess?
    A. Legitimate    B. Reward    C. Referent    D. Expert

# KEY (CORRECT ANSWERS)

1. C
2. B
3. A
4. D
5. A

6. B
7. C
8. D
9. B
10. D

11. A
12. C
13. D
14. C
15. A

16. D
17. C
18. B
19. D
20. A

21. C
22. C
23. B
24. A
25. D

# EXAMINATION SECTION
## TEST 1

DIRECTIONS: Each question or incomplete statement is followed by several suggested answers or completions. Select the one that BEST answers the question or completes the statement. *PRINT THE LETTER OF THE CORRECT ANSWER IN THE SPACE AT THE RIGHT.*

1. In public agencies, communications should be based PRIMARILY on a
   A. two-way flow from the top down and from the bottom up, most of which should be given in writing to avoid ambiguity
   B. multi-direction flow among all levels and with outside persons
   C. rapid, internal one-way flow from the top down
   D. two-way flow of information, most of which should be given orally for purposes of clarity

   1.____

2. In some organizations, changes in policy or procedures are often communicated by word of mouth from supervisors to employees with no prior discussion or exchange of viewpoints with employees.
   This procedure often produces employee dissatisfaction CHIEFLY because
   A. information is mostly unusable since a considerable amount of time is required to transmit information
   B. lower-level supervisors tend to be excessively concerned with minor details
   C. management has failed to seek employees' advice before making changes
   D. valuable staff time is lost between decision-making and the implementation of decisions

   2.____

3. For good letter writing, you should try to visualize the person to whom you are writing, especially if you know him.
   Of the following rules, it is LEAST helpful in such visualization to think of
   A. the person's likes and dislikes, his concerns, and his needs
   B. what you would be likely to say if speaking in person
   C. what you would expect to be asked if speaking in person
   D. your official position in order to be certain that your words are proper

   3.____

4. One approach to good informal letter writing is to make letters and conversational.
   All of the following practices will usually help to do this EXCEPT:
   A. If possible, use a style which is similar to the style used when speaking
   B. Substitute phrases for single words (e.g., *at the present time* for *now*)
   C. Use contractions of words (e.g., *you're* for *you are*)
   D. Use ordinary vocabulary when possible

   4.____

5. All of the following rules will aid in producing clarity in report-writing EXCEPT:
   A. Give specific details or examples, if possible
   B. Keep related words close together in each sentence
   C. Present information in sequential order
   D. Put several thoughts or ideas in each paragraph

6. The one of the following statements about public relations which is MOST accurate is that
   A. in the long run, appearance gains better results than performance
   B. objectivity is decreased if outside public relations consultants are employed
   C. public relations is the responsibility of every employee
   D. public relations should be based on a formal publicity program

7. The form of communication which is usually considered to be MOST personally directed to the intended recipient is the
   A. brochure   B. film   C. letter   D. radio

8. In general, a document that presents an organization's views or opinions on a particular topic is MOST accurately known as a
   A. tear sheet         B. position paper
   C. flyer              D. journal

9. Assume that you have been asked to speak before an organization of persons who oppose a newly announced program in which you are involved. You feel tense about talking to this group.
   Which of the following rules generally would be MOST useful in gaining rapport when speaking before the audience?
   A. Impress them with your experience
   B. Stress all areas of disagreement
   C. Talk to the group as to one person
   D. Use formal grammar and language

10. An organization must have an effective public relations program since, at its best, public relations is a bridge to change.
    All of the following statements about communication and human behavior have validity EXCEPT:
    A. People are more likely to talk about controversial matters with like-minded people than with those holding other views
    B. The earlier an experience, the more powerful its effect since it influences how later experiences will be interpreted
    C. In periods of social tension, official sources gain increased believability
    D. Those who are already interested in a topic are the ones who are most open to receive new communications about it

11. An employee should be encouraged to talk easily and frankly when he is dealing with his supervisor.
    In order to encourage such free communication, it would be MOST appropriate for a supervisor to behave in a(n)
    A. sincere manner; assure the employee that you will deal with him honestly and openly
    B. official manner; you are a supervisor and must always act formally with subordinates
    C. investigative manner; you must probe and question to get to a basis of trust
    D. unemotional manner; the employee's emotions and background should play no part in your dealings with him

11._____

12. Research findings show that an increase in free communication within an agency GENERALLY results in which one of the following?
    A. Improved morale and productivity
    B. Increased promotional opportunities
    C. An increase in authority
    D. A spirit of honesty

12._____

13. Assume that you are a supervisor and your superiors have given you a new-type procedure to be followed.
    Before passing this information on to your subordinates, the one of the following actions that you should take FIRST is to
    A. ask your superiors to send out a memorandum to the entire staff
    B. clarify the procedure in your own mind
    C. set up a training course to provide instruction on the new procedure
    D. write a memorandum to your subordinates

13._____

14. Communication is necessary for an organization to be effective.
    The one of the following which is LEAST important for most communication systems is that
    A. messages are sent quickly and directly to the person who needs them to operate
    B. information should be conveyed understandably and accurately
    C. the method used to transmit information should be kept secret so that security can be maintained
    D. senders of messages must know how their messages are received and acted upon

14._____

15. Which one of the following is the CHIEF advantage of listening willingly to subordinates and encouraging them to talk freely and honestly?
    It
    A. reveals to supervisors the degree to which ideas that are passed down are accepted by subordinates
    B. reduces the participation of subordinates in the operation of the department
    C. encourages subordinates to try for promotion
    D. enables supervisors to learn more readily what the *grapevine* is saying

15._____

16. A supervisor may be informed through either oral or written reports. 16.____
Which one of the following is an ADVANTAGE of using oral reports?
    A. There is no need for a formal record of the report.
    B. An exact duplicate of the report is not easily transmitted to others.
    C. A good oral report requires little time for preparation.
    D. An oral report involves two-way communication between a subordinate and his supervisor.

17. Of the following, the MOST important reason why supervisors should 17.____
communicate effectively with the public is to
    A. improve the public's understanding of information that is important for them to know
    B. establish a friendly relationship
    C. obtain information about the kinds of people who come to the agency
    D. convince the public that services are adequate

18. Supervisors should generally NOT use phrases like *too hard*, *too easy*, and 18.____
*a lot* PRINCIPALLY because such phrases
    A. may be offensive to some minority groups
    B. are too informal
    C. mean different things to different people
    D. are difficult to remember

19. The ability to communicate clearly and concisely is an important element in 19.____
effective leadership.
Which of the following statements about oral and written communication is GENERALLY true?
    A. Oral communication is more time-consuming.
    B. Written communication is more likely to be misinterpreted.
    C. Oral communication is useful only in emergencies.
    D. Written communication is useful mainly when giving information to fewer than twenty people.

20. Rumors can often have harmful and disruptive effects on an organization. 20.____
Which one of the following is the BEST way to prevent rumors from becoming a problem?
    A. Refuse to act on rumors, thereby making them less believable.
    B. Increase the amount of information passed along by the *grapevine*.
    C. Distribute as much factual information as possible.
    D. Provide training in report writing.

21. Suppose that a subordinate asks you about a rumor he has heard. The rumor 21.____
deals with a subject which your superiors consider *confidential*.
Which of the following BEST describes how you should answer the subordinate? Tell

A. the subordinate that you don't make the rules and that he should speak to higher ranking officials
B. the subordinate that you will ask your superior for information
C. him only that you cannot comment on the matter
D. him the rumor is not true

22. Supervisors often find it difficult to *get their message across* when instructing newly appointed employees in their various duties.
The MAIN reason for this is generally that the
   A. duties of the employees have increased
   B. supervisor is often so expert in his area that he fails to see it from the learner's point of view
   C. supervisor adapts his instruction to the slowest learner in the group
   D. new employees are younger, less concerned with job security and more interested in fringe benefits

22.____

23. Assume that you are discussing a job problem with an employee under your supervision. During the discussion, you see that the man's eyes are turning away from you and that he is not paying attention.
In order to get the man's attention, you should FIRST
   A. ask him to look you in the eye
   B. talk to him about sports
   C. tell him he is being very rude
   D. change your tone of voice

23.____

24. As a supervisor, you may find it necessary to conduct meetings with your subordinates.
Of the following, which would be MOST helpful in assuring that a meeting accomplishes the purpose for which it was called?
   A. Give notice of the conclusions you would like to reach at the start of the meeting.
   B. Delay the start of the meeting until everyone is present.
   C. Write down points to be discussed in proper sequence.
   D. Make sure everyone is clear on whatever conclusions have been reached and on what must be done after the meeting.

24.____

25. Every supervisor will occasionally be called upon to deliver a reprimand to a subordinate. If done properly, this can greatly help an employee improve his performance.
Which one of the following is NOT a good practice to follow when giving a reprimand?
   A. Maintain your composure and temper
   B. Reprimand a subordinate in the presence of other employees so they can learn the same lesson
   C. Try to understand why the employee was not able to perform satisfactorily
   D. Let your knowledge of the man involved determine the exact nature of the reprimand

25.____

## KEY (CORRECT ANSWERS)

| | | | | |
|---|---|---|---|---|
| 1. | C | | 11. | A |
| 2. | B | | 12. | A |
| 3. | D | | 13. | B |
| 4. | B | | 14. | C |
| 5. | D | | 15. | A |
| | | | | |
| 6. | C | | 16. | D |
| 7. | C | | 17. | A |
| 8. | B | | 18. | C |
| 9. | C | | 19. | B |
| 10. | C | | 20. | C |

21. B
22. B
23. D
24. D
25. B

# TEST 2

DIRECTIONS: Each question or incomplete statement is followed by several suggested answers or completions. Select the one that BEST answers the question or completes the statement. *PRINT THE LETTER OF THE CORRECT ANSWER IN THE SPACE AT THE RIGHT.*

1. Usually one thinks of communication as a single step, essentially that of transmitting an idea.
   Actually, however, this is only part of a total process, the FIRST step of which should be
   A. the prompt dissemination of the idea to those who may be affected by it
   B. motivating those affected to take the required action
   C. clarifying the idea in one's own mind
   D. deciding to whom the idea is to be communicated

   1.____

2. Research studies on patterns of informal communication have concluded that most individuals in a group tend to be passive recipients of news, while a few make it their business to spread it around in an organization.
   With this conclusion in mind, it would be MOST correct for the supervisor to attempt to identify these few individuals and
   A. give them the complete facts on important matters in advance of others
   B. inform the other subordinates of the identity of these few individuals so that their influence may be minimized
   C. keep them straight on the facts on important matters
   D. warn them to cease passing along any information to others

   2.____

3. The one of the following which is the PRINCIPAL advantage of making an oral report is that it
   A. affords an immediate opportunity for two-way communication between the subordinate and superior
   B. is an easy method for the superior to use in transmitting information to others of equal rank
   C. saves the time of all concerned
   D. permits more precise pinpointing of praise or blame by means of follow-up questions by the superior

   3.____

4. An agency may sometimes undertake a public relations program of a defensive nature.
   With reference to the use of defensive public relations, it would be MOST correct to state that it
   A. is bound to be ineffective since defensive statements, even though supported by factual data, can never hope to even partly overcome the effects of prior unfavorable attacks
   B. proves that the agency has failed to establish good relationships with newspapers, radio stations, or other means of publicity

   4.____

C. shows that the upper echelons of the agency have failed to develop sound public relations procedures and techniques
D. is sometimes required to aid morale by protecting the agency from unjustified criticism and misunderstanding of policies or procedures

5. Of the following factors which contribute to possible undesirable public attitudes towards an agency, the one which is MOST susceptible to being changed by the efforts of the individual employee in an organization is that
    A. enforcement of unpopular regulations as offended many individuals
    B. the organization itself has an unsatisfactory reputation
    C. the public is not interested in agency matters
    D. there are many errors in judgment committed by individual subordinates

6. It is not enough for an agency's services to be of a high quality; attention must also be given to the acceptability of these services to the general public.
This statement is GENERALLY
    A. *false*; a superior quality of service automatically wins public support
    B. *true*; the agency cannot generally progress beyond the understanding and support of the public
    C. *false*; the acceptance by the public of agency services determines their quality
    D. *true*; the agency is generally unable to engage in any effective enforcement activity without public support

7. Sustained agency participation in a program sponsored by a community organization is MOST justified when
    A. the achievement of agency objectives in some area depends partly on the activity of this organization
    B. the community organization is attempting to widen the base of participation in all community affairs
    C. the agency is uncertain as to what the community wants
    D. the agency is uncertain as to what the community wants

8. Of the following, the LEAST likely way in which a records system may serve a supervisor is in
    A. developing a sympathetic and cooperative public attitude toward the agency
    B. improving the quality of supervision by permitting a check on the accomplishment of subordinates
    C. permit a precise prediction of the exact incidences in specific categories for the following year
    D. helping to take the guesswork out of the distribution of the agency

9. Assuming that the *grapevine* in any organization is virtually indestructible, the one of the following which it is MOST important for management to understand is:
    A. What is being spread by means of the *grapevine* and the reason for spreading it
    B. What is being spread by means of the *grapevine* and how it is being spread
    C. Who is involved in spreading the information that is on the *grapevine*
    D. Why those who are involved in spreading the information are doing so

10. When the supervisor writes a report concerning an investigation to which he has been assigned, it should be LEAST intended to provide
    A. a permanent official record of relevant information gathered
    B. a summary of case findings limited to facts which tend to indicate the guilt of a suspect
    C. a statement of the facts on which higher authorities may base a corrective or disciplinary action
    D. other investigators with information so that they may continue with other phases of the investigation

11. In survey work, questionnaires rather than interviews are sometimes used. The one of the following which is a DISADVANTAGE of the questionnaire method as compared with the interview is the
    A. difficulty of accurately interpreting the results
    B. problem of maintaining anonymity of the participant
    C. fact that it is relatively uneconomical
    D. requirement of special training for the distribution of questionnaires

12. in his contacts with the public, an employee should attempt to create a good climate of support for his agency.
    This statement is GENERALLY
    A. *false*; such attempts are clearly beyond the scope of his responsibility
    B. *true*; employees of an agency who come in contact with the public have the opportunity to affect public relations
    C. *false*; such activity should be restricted to supervisors trained in public relations techniques
    D. *true*; the future expansion of the agency depends to a great extent on continued public support of the agency

13. The repeated use by a supervisor of a call for volunteers to get a job done is objectionable MAINLY because it
    A. may create a feeling of animosity between the volunteers and the non-volunteers
    B. may indicate that the supervisor is avoiding responsibility for making assignments which will be most productive
    C. is an indication that the supervisor is not familiar with the individual capabilities of his men
    D. is unfair to men who, for valid reasons, do not, or cannot volunteer

14. Of the following statements concerning subordinates' expressions to a supervisor of their opinions and feelings concerning work situations, the one which is MOST correct is that
    A. by listening and responding to such expressions the supervisor encourages the development of complaints
    B. the lack of such expressions should indicate to the supervisor that there is a high level of job satisfaction
    C. the more the supervisor listens to and responds to such expressions, the more he demonstrates lack of supervisory ability
    D. by listening and responding to such expressions, the supervisor will enable many subordinates to understand and solve their own problems on the job

14._____

15. In attempting to motivate employees, rewards are considered preferable to punishment PRIMARILY because
    A. punishment seldom has any effect on human behavior
    B. punishment usually results in decreased production
    C. supervisors find it difficult to punish
    D. rewards are more likely to result in willing cooperation

15._____

16. In an attempt to combat the low morale in his organization, a high level supervisor publicized an *open-door policy* to allow employees who wished to do so to come to him with their complaints.
    Which of the following is LEAST likely to account for the fact that no employee came in with a complaint?
    A. Employees are generally reluctant to go over the heads of their immediate supervisor.
    B. The employees did not feel that management would help them.
    C. The low morale was not due to complaints associated with the job.
    D. The employees felt that they had more to lose than to gain.

16._____

17. It is MOST desirable to use written instructions rather than oral instructions for a particular job when
    A. a mistake on the job will not be serious
    B. the job can be completed in a short time
    C. there is no need to explain the job minutely
    D. the job involves many details

17._____

18. If you receive a telephone call regarding a matter which your office does not handle, you should FIRST
    A. give the caller the telephone number of the proper office so that he can dial again
    B. offer to transfer the caller to the proper office
    C. suggest that the caller re-dial since he probably dialed incorrectly
    D. tell the caller he has reached the wrong office and then hang up

18._____

19. When you answer the telephone, the MOST important reason for identifying yourself and your organization is to
    A. give the caller time to collect his or her thoughts
    B. impress the caller with your courtesy
    C. inform the caller that he or she has reached the right number
    D. set a business-like tone at the beginning of the conversation

19.____

20. As soon as you pick up the phone, a very angry caller begins immediately to complain about city agencies and *red tape*. He says that he has been shifted to two or three different offices. It turs out that he is seeking information which is not immediately available to you. You believe, you know, however, where it can be found.
    Which of the following actions is the BEST one for you to take?
    A. To eliminate all confusion, suggest that the caller write the agency stating explicitly what he wants.
    B. Apologize by telling the caller how busy city agencies now are, but also tell him directly that you do not have the information he needs.
    C. Ask for the caller's telephone number and assure him you will call back after you have checked further.
    D. Give the caller the name and telephone number of the person who might be able to help, but explain that you are not positive he will get results/

20.____

21. Which of the following approaches usually provides the BEST communication in the objectives and values of a new program which is to be introduced?
    A. A general written description of the program by the program manager for review by those who share responsibility
    B. An effective verbal presentation by the program manager to those affected
    C. Development of the plan and operational approach in carrying out the program by the program manager assisted by his key subordinates
    D. Development of the plan by the program manager's supervisor

21.____

22. What is the BEST approach for introducing change?
    A
    A. combination of written and also verbal communication to all personnel affected by the change
    B. general bulletin to all personnel
    C. meeting pointing out all the values of the new approach
    D. written directive to key personnel

22.____

23. Of the following, committees are BEST used for
    A. advising the head of the organization
    B. improving functional work
    C. making executive decisions
    D. making specific planning decisions

23.____

24. An effective discussion leader is one who
    A. announces the problem and his preconceived solution at the start of the discussion
    B. guides and directs the discussion according to pre-arranged outline
    C. interrupts or corrects confused participants to save time
    D. permits anyone to say anything at any time

25. The human relations movement in management theory is basically concerned with
    A. counteracting employee unrest
    B. eliminating the *time and motion* man
    C. interrelationships among individuals in organizations
    D. the psychology of the worker

# KEY (CORRECT ANSWERS)

| | | | |
|---|---|---|---|
| 1. | C | 11. | A |
| 2. | C | 12. | B |
| 3. | A | 13. | B |
| 4. | D | 14. | D |
| 5. | D | 15. | D |
| 6. | B | 16. | C |
| 7. | A | 17. | D |
| 8. | C | 18. | B |
| 9. | A | 19. | C |
| 10. | B | 20. | C |

| | |
|---|---|
| 21. | C |
| 22. | A |
| 23. | A |
| 24. | B |
| 25. | C |

# SUPERVISION STUDY GUIDE

Social science has developed information about groups and leadership in general and supervisor-employee relationships in particular. Since organizational effectiveness is closely linked to the ability of supervisors to direct the activities of employees, these findings are important to executives everywhere.

IS A SUPERVISOR A LEADER?

First-line supervisors are found in all large business and government organizations. They are the men at the base of an organizational hierarchy. Decisions made by the head of the organization reach them through a network of intermediate positions. They are frequently referred to as part of the management team, but their duties seldom seem to support this description.

A supervisor of clerks, tax collectors, meat inspectors, or securities analysts is not charged with budget preparation. He cannot hire or fire the employees in his own unit on his say-so. He does not administer programs which require great planning, coordinating, or decision making.

Then what is he? He is the man who is directly in charge of a group of employees doing productive work for a business or government agency. If the work requires the use of machines, the men he supervises operate them. If the work requires the writing of reports, the men he supervises write them. He is expected to maintain a productive flow of work without creating problems which higher levels of management must solve. But is he a leader?

To carry out a specific part of an agency's mission, management creates a unit, staffs it with a group of employees and designates a supervisor to take charge of them. Management directs what this unit shall do, from time to time changes directions, and often indicates what the group should not do. Management presumably creates status for the supervisor by giving him more pay, a title, and special privileges.

Management asks a supervisor to get his workers to attain organizational goals, including the desired quantity and quality of production. Supposedly, he has authority to enable him to achieve this objective. Management at least assumes that by establishing the status of the supervisor's position, it has created sufficient authority to enable him to achieve these goals—not his goals, nor necessarily the group's, but management's goals.

In addition, supervision includes writing reports, keeping records of membership in a higher-level administrative group, industrial engineering, safety engineering, editorial duties, housekeeping duties, etc. The supervisor as a member of an organizational network, must be responsible to the changing demands of the management above him. At the same time, he must be responsive to the demands of the work group of which he is a member. He is placed in the difficult position of communicating and implementing new decisions, changed programs and revised production quotas for his work group, although he may have had little part in developing them.

It follows, then, that supervision has a special characteristic: achievement of goals, previously set by management, through the efforts of others. It is in this feature of the supervisor's job that we find the role of a leader in the sense of the following definition: *A leader is that person who most effectively influences group activities toward goal setting and goal achievements.*

This definition is broad. It covers both leaders in groups that come together voluntarily and in those brought together through a work assignment in a factory, store, or government agency. In the natural group, the authority necessary to attain goals is determined by the group membership and is granted by them. In the working group, it is apparent that the establishment of a supervisory position creates a predisposition on the part of employees to accept the authority of the occupant of that position. We cannot, however, assume that mere occupation confers authority sufficient to assure the accomplishment of an organization's goals.

Supervision is different, then, from leadership. The supervisor is expected to fulfill the role of leader but without obtaining a grant of authority from the group he supervises. The supervisor is expected to influence the group in the achieving of goals but is often handicapped by having little influence on the organizational process by which goals are set. The supervisor, because he works in an organizational setting, has the burdens of additional organizational duties and restrictions and requirements arising out of the fact that his position is subordinate to a hierarchy of higher-level supervisors. These differences between leadership and supervision are reflected in our definition: *Supervision is basically a leadership role, in a formal organization, which has as its objective the effective influencing of other employees.*

Even though these differences between supervision and leadership exist, a significant finding of experimenters in this field is that supervisors must be leaders to be successful.

The problem is: How can a supervisor exercise leadership in an organizational setting? We might say that the supervisor is expected to be a natural leader in a situation which does not come about naturally. His situation becomes really difficult in an organization which is more eager to make its supervisors into followers rather than leaders.

LEADERSHIP: NATURAL AND ORGANIZATIONAL

Leadership, in its usual sense of *natural* leadership, and supervision are not the same. In some cases, leadership embraces broader powers and functions than supervision; in other cases, supervision embraces more than leadership. This is true both because of the organization and technical aspects of the supervisor's job and because of the relatively freer setting and inherent authority of the natural leader.

The natural leader usually has much more authority and influence than the supervisor. Group members not only follow his command but prefer it that way. The employee, however, can appeal the supervisor's commands to his union or to the supervisor's superior or to the personnel office. These intercessors represent restrictions on the supervisor's power to lead.

The natural leader can gain greater membership involvement in the group's objectives, and he can change the objectives of the group. The supervisor can attempt to gain employee support only for management's objectives; he cannot set other objectives. In these instances leadership is broader than supervision.

The natural leader must depend upon whatever skills are available when seeking to attain objectives. The supervisor is trained in the administrative skills necessary to achieve management's goals. If he does not possess the requisite skills, however, he can call upon management's technicians.

A natural leader can maintain his leadership, in certain groups, merely by satisfying members' need for group affiliation. The supervisor must maintain his leadership by directing and organizing his group to achieve specific organizational goals set for him and his group by management. He must have a technical competence and a kind of coordinating ability which is not needed by many natural leaders.

A natural leader is responsible only to his group which grants him authority. The supervisor is responsible to management, which employs him, and also to the work group of which he is a member. The supervisor has the exceedingly difficult job of reconciling the demands of two groups frequently in conflict. He is often placed in the untenable position of trying to play two antagonistic roles. In the above instance, supervision is broader than leadership.

ORGANIZATIONAL INFLUENCES ON LEADERSHIP

The supervisor is both a product and a prisoner of the organization wherein we find him. The organization which creates the supervisor's position also obstructs, restricts, and channelizes the exercise of his duties. These influences extend beyond prescribed functional relationships to specific supervisory behavior. For example, even in a face-to-face situation involving one of his subordinates, the supervisor's actions are controlled to a great extent by his organization. His behavior must conform to the organization policy on human relations, rules which dictate personnel procedures, specific prohibitions governing conduct, the attitudes of his own superior, etc. He is not a free agent operating within the limits of his work group. His freedom of action is much more circumscribed than is generally admitted. The organizational influences which limit his leadership actions can be classified as structure, prescriptions, and proscriptions.

The organizational structure places each supervisor's position in context with other designated positions. It determines the relationships between his position and specific positions which impinge on his. The structure of the organization designates a certain position to which he looks for orders and information about his work. It gives a particular status to his position within a pattern of statuses from which he perceives that (1) certain positions are on a par, organizationally, with his, (2) other positions are subordinate, and (3) still others are superior.

The organizational structure determines those positions to which he should look for advice and assistance, and those positions to which he should give advice and assistance.

For instance, the organizational structure has predetermined that the supervisor of a clerical processing unit shall report to a supervisory position in a higher echelon. He shall have certain relationships with the supervisors of the work units which transmit work to and receive work from his unit. He shall discuss changes and clarification of procedures with certain staff units, such as organization and methods, cost accounting, and personnel. He shall consult supervisors of units which provide or receive special work assignments.

The organizational structure, however, establishes patterns other than those of the relationships of positions. These are the patterns of responsibility, authority, and expectations.

The supervisor is responsible for certain activities or results; he is presumably invested with the authority to achieve these. His set of authority and responsibility is interwoven with other sets to the end that all goals and functions of the organization are parceled out in small, manageable lots. This, of course, establishes a series of expectations: a single supervisor can perform his particular set of duties only upon the assumption that preceding or contiguous sets of duties have been, or are being carried out. At the same time, he is aware of the expectations of others that he will fulfill his functional role.

The structure of an organization establishes relationships between specified positions and specific expectations for these positions. The fact that these relationships and expectations are established is one thing; whether or not they are met is another.

PRESCRIPTIONS AND PROSCRIPTIONS

But let us return to the organizational influences which act to restrict the supervisor's exercise of leadership. These are the prescriptions and proscriptions generally in effect in all organizations, and those peculiar to a single organization. In brief these are the *thou shalt's* and the *thou shalt not's*.

Organizations not only prescribe certain duties for individual supervisory positions, they also prescribe specific methods and means of carrying out these duties and maintaining management-employee relations. These include rules, regulations, policy, and tradition. It does no good for the supervisor to say, *This seems to be the best way to handle such-and-such,* if the organization has established a routine for dealing with problems. For good or bad, there are rules that state that firings shall be executed in such a manner, accompanied by a certain notification; that training shall be conducted, and in this manner. Proscriptions are merely negative prescriptions; you may not discriminate against any employee because of politics or race; you shall not suspend any employee without following certain procedures and obtaining certain approvals.

Most of these prohibitions and rules apply to the area of interpersonal relations, precisely the area which is now arousing most interest on the part of administrators and managers. We have become concerned about the contrast between formally prescribed relationships and interpersonal relationships, and this brings us to the often discussed informal organization.

# FORMAL AND INFORMAL ORGANIZATIONS

As we well know, the functions and activities of any organization are broken down into individual units of work called positions. Administrators must establish a pattern which will link these positions to each other and relate them to a system of authority and responsibility. Man-to-man are spelled out as plainly as possible for all to understand. Managers, then, build an official structure which we call the formal organization.

In these same organizations, employees react individually and in groups to institutionally determined roles. John, a worker, rides in the same carpool as Joe, a foreman. An unplanned communication develops. Harry, a machinist knows more about high-speed machining than his foreman or anyone else in his shop. An unofficial tool boss comes into being. Mary, who fought with Jane, is promoted over her. Jane now gives Mary's directions. A planned relationship fails to develop. The employees have built a structure which we call the informal organization.

> *Formal organization is a system of management-prescribed relations between positions in an organization.*
>
> *Informal organization is a network of unofficial relations between people in an organization.*

These definitions might lead us to the absurd conclusion that positions carry out formal activities and that employe4es spend their time in unofficial activities. We must recognize that organizational activities are in all cases carried out by people. The formal structure provides a needed framework within which interpersonal relations occur. What we call informal organization is the complex of normal, natural relations among employees. These personal relationships may be negative or positive. That is, they may impede or aid the achievement of organizational goals. For example, friendship between two supervisors greatly increases the probability of good cooperation and coordination between their sections. On the other hand, *buck passing* nullifies the formal structure by failure to meet a prescribed and expected responsibility.

It is improbable that an ideal organization exists where all activities are carried out in strict conformity to a formally prescribed pattern of functional roles. Informal organization arises because of the incompleteness and ambiguities in the network of formally prescribed relationships, or in response to the needs or inadequacies of supervisors or managers who hold prescribed functional roles in an organization. Many of these relationships are not prescribed by the organizational pattern; many cannot be prescribed; many should not be prescribed.

Management faces the problem of keeping the informal organization in harmony with the mission of the agency. One way to do this is to make sure that all employees have a clear understanding of and are sympathetic with that mission. The issuance of organizational charts, procedural manuals, and functional descriptions of the work to be done by divisions and sections helps communicate management's plans and goals. Issuances alone, of course, cannot do the whole job. They should be accompanied by oral discussion and explanation. Management must ensure that there is mutual understanding and acceptance of charts and procedures. More important is that management acquaint itself with the attitudes, activities, and peculiar brands of logic which govern the informal organization. Only through this type of knowledge can they and supervisors keep informal goals consistent with the agency mission.

## SUPERVISION STATUS AND FUNCTIONAL ROLE

A well-established supervisor is respected by the employees who work with him. They defer to his wishes. It is clear that a superior-subordinate relationship has been established. That is, status of the supervisor has been established in relation to other employees of the same work group. This same supervisor gains the respect of employees when he behaves in as certain manner. He will be expected, generally, to follow the customs of the group in such matters as dress, recreation, and manner of speaking. The group has a set of expectations as to his behavior. His position is a functional role which carries with it a collection of rights and obligations.

The position of supervisor usually has a status distinct from the individual who occupies it: it is much like a position description which exists whether or not there is an incumbent. The status of a supervisory position is valued higher than that of an employee position both because of the functional role of leadership which is assigned to it and because of the status symbols of titles, rights, and privileges which go with it.

Social ranking, or status, is not simple because it involves both the position and the man. An individual may be ranked higher than others because of his education, social background, perceived leadership ability, or conformity to group customs and ideals. If such a man is ranked higher by the members of a work group than their supervisor, the supervisor's effectiveness may be seriously undermined.

If the organization does not build and reinforce a supervisor's status, his position can be undermined in a different way. This will happen when managers go around rather than through the supervisor or designate him as a straw boss, acting boss, or otherwise not a real boss.

Let us clarify this last point. A role, and corresponding status, establishes a set of expectations. Employees expect their supervisor to do certain things and to act in certain ways. They are prepared to respond to that expected behavior. When the supervisor's behavior does not conform to their expectations, they are surprised, confused, and ill-at-ease. It becomes necessary for them to resolve their confusion, if they can. They might do this by turning to one of their own members for leadership. If the confusion continues, or their attempted solutions are not satisfactory, they will probably become a poorly motivated, non-cohesive group which cannot function very well.

## COMMUNICATION AND THE SUPERVISOR

In a recent survey, railroad workers reported that they rarely look to their supervisor for information about the company. This is startling, at least to us, because we ordinarily think of the supervisor as the link between management and worker. We expect the supervisor to be the prime source of information about the company. Actually, the railroad workers listed the supervisor next to last in the o5rder of their sources of information. Most surprising of all, the supervisors, themselves, stated that rumor and unofficial contacts were their principal sources of information. Here we see one of the reasons why supervisors may not be as effective as management desires.

The supervisor is not only being bypassed by his work group, he is being ignored, and his position weakened, by the very organization which is holding him responsible for the activities of his workers. If he is management's representative to the employee, then management has an obligation to keep him informed of its activities. This is necessary if he is to carry out his functions efficiently and maintain his leadership in the work group. The supervisor is expected to be a source of information; when he is not, his status is not clear, and employees are dissatisfied because he has not lived up to expectations.

By providing information to the supervisor to pass along to employees, we can strengthen his position as leader of the group, and increase satisfaction and cohesion within the group. Because he has more information than the other members, receives information sooner, and passes it along at the proper times, members turn to him as a source and also provide him with information in the hope of receiving some in return. From this, we can see an increase in group cohesiveness because:

- Employees are bound closer to their supervisor because he is *in the know*.
- There is less need to go outside the group for answers
- Employees will more quickly turn to the supervisor for enlightenment

The fact that he has the answers will also enhance the supervisor's standing in the eyes of his men. This increased status will serve to bolster his authority and control of the group and will probably result in improved morale and productivity.

The foregoing, of course, does not mean that all management information should be given out. There are obviously certain policy determinations and discussions which need not or cannot be transmitted to all supervisors. However, the supervisor must be kept as fully informed as possible so that he can answer questions when asked and can allay needless fears and anxieties. Further, the supervisor has the responsibility of encouraging employee questions and submissions of information. He must be able to present information to employees so that it is clearly understood and accepted. His attitude and manner should make it clear that he believes in what he is saying, that the information is necessary or desirable to the group, and that he is prepared to act on the basis of the information.

SUPERVISION AND JOB PERFORMANCE

The productivity of work groups is a product; employees' efforts are multiplied by the supervision they receive. Many investigators have analyzed this relationship and have discovered elements of supervision which differentiate high and low production groups. These researchers have identified certain types of supervisory practices which they classify as *employee-centered* and other types which they classify as *production centered*.

The difference between these two kinds of supervision lies not in specific practices but in the approach or orientation to supervision. The employee-centered supervisor directs most of his efforts toward increasing employee motivation. He is concerned more with realizing the potential energy of persons than with administrative and technological methods of increasing efficiency and productivity. He is the man who finds ways of causing employees to want to work harder with the same tools. These supervisors emphasize the personal relations between their employees and themselves.

Now, obviously, these pictures are overdrawn. No one supervisor has all the virtues of the ideal type of employee-centered supervisor. And, fortunately, no one supervisor has all the bad traits found in many production-centered supervisors. We should remember that the various practices that researchers have fond which distinguish these two kinds of supervision represent the many practices and methods of supervisors of all gradations between these extremes. We should be careful, too, of the implications of the labels attached to the two types. For instance, being production-centered is not necessarily bad, since the principal responsibility of any supervisor is maintaining the production level that is expected of his work group. Being employee-centered may not necessarily be good, if the only result is a happy, chuckling crew of loafers. To return to the researchers' findings, employee-centered supervisors:

- Recommend promotions, transfers, pay increases
- Inform men about what is happening in the company
- Keep men posted on how well they are doing
- Hear complaints and grievances sympathetically
- Speak up for subordinates

Production-centered supervisors, on the other hand, don't do those things. They check on employees more frequently, give more detailed and frequent instructions, don't give reasons for changes, and are more punitive when mistakes are made. Employee-centered supervisors were reported to contribute to high morale and high production, whereas production-centered supervision was associated with lower morale and less production.

More recent findings, however, show that the relationship between supervision and productivity is not this simple. Investigators now report that high production is more frequently associated with supervisory practices which combine employee-centered behavior with concern for production. (This concern is not the same, however, as anxiety about production, which is the hallmark of our production-centered supervisor.) Let us examine these apparently contradictory findings and the premises from which they are derived.

SUPERVISION AND MORALE

Why do supervisory activities cause high or low production? As the name implies, the activities of the employee-centered supervisor tend to relate him more closely and satisfactorily to his workers. The production-centered supervisor's practices tend to separate him from his group and to foster antagonism. An analysis of this difference may answer our question.

Earlier, we pointed out that the supervisor is a type of leader and that leadership is intimately related to the group in which it occurs We discover, now, that an employee-centered supervisor's primary activities are concerned with both his leadership and his group membership. Such a supervisor is a member of a group and occupies a leadership role in that group.

These facts are sometimes obscured when we speak of the supervisor as management's representative, or as the organizational link between management and the employee, or as the end of the chain of command. If we really want to understand what it is we expect of the supervisor, we must remember that he is the designated leader of a group of employees to whom he is bound by interaction and interdependence.

Most of his actions are aimed, consciously or unconsciously, at strengthening membership ties in the group. This includes both making members more conscious that he is a member of their group) and causing members to identify themselves more closely with the group. These ends are accomplished by:

- making the group more attractive to the worker: they find satisfaction of their needs for recognition, friendship, enjoyable work, etc.;
- maintaining open communication: employees can express their views and obtain information about the organization
- giving assistance: members can seek advice on personal problems as well as their work; and
- acting as a buffer between the group and management: he speaks up for his men and explains the reasons for management's decisions.

Such actions both strengthen group cohesiveness and solidarity and affirm the supervisor's leadership position in the group.

DEFINING MORALE

This brings us back to a point mentioned earlier. We had said that employee-centered supervisors contribute to high morale as well as to high production. But how can we explain units which have low morale and high productivity, or vice versa? Usually production and morale are considered separately, partly because they are measured against different criteria and partly because, in some instances, they seem to be independent of each other.

Some of this difficulty may stem from confusion over definitions of morale. Morale has been defined as, or measured by, absences from work, satisfaction with job or company, dissension among members of work groups, productivity, apathy or lack of interest, readiness to help others, and a general aura of happiness as rated by observers. Some of these criteria of morale are not subject to the influence of the supervisor, and some of them are not clearly related to productivity. Definitions like these invite findings of low morale coupled with high production.

Both productivity and morale can be influenced by environmental factors not under the control of group members or supervisors. Such things as plant layout, organizational structure and goals, lighting, ventilation, communications, and management planning may have an adverse or desirable effect.

We might resolve the dilemma by defining morale on the basis of our understanding of the supervisor as leader of a group; morale is the degree of satisfaction of group members with their leadership. In this light, the supervisor's employee-centered activities bear a clear relation to morale. His efforts to increase employee identification with the group and to strengthen his leadership lead to greater satisfaction with that leadership. By increasing group cohesiveness and by demonstrating that his influence and power can aid the group, he is able to enhance his leadership status and afford satisfaction to the group.

SUPERVISION, PRODUCTION, AND MORALE

There are factors within the organization itself which determine whether increased production is possible:

- Are production goals expressed in terms understandable to employees and are they realistic?
- Do supervisors responsible for production respect the agency mission and production goals?
- If employees do not know how to do the job well, does management provide a trainer—often the supervisor—who can teach efficient work methods?

There are other factors within the work group which determine whether increased production will be attained:

- Is leadership present which can bring about the desired level of production?
- Are production goals accepted by employees as reasonable and attainable?
- If group effort is involved, are members able to coordinate their efforts?

Research findings confirm the view that an employee-centered supervisor can achieve higher morale than a production-centered supervisor. Managers may well ask what is the relationship between this and production.

Supervision is production-oriented to the extent that it focuses attention on achieving organizational goals, and plans and devises methods for attaining them; it is employee-centered to the extent that it focuses attention on employee attitudes toward those goals, and plans and works toward maintenance of employee satisfaction.

High productivity and low morale result when a supervisor plans and organizes work efficiently but cannot achieve high membership satisfaction. Low production and high morale result when a supervisor, though keeping members satisfied with his leadership, either has not gained acceptance of organizational goals or does not have the technical competence to achieve them.

The relationship between supervision, morale, and productivity is an interdependent one, with the supervisor playing an integral role due to his ability to influence productivity and morale independently of each other.

A supervisor who can plan his work well has good technical knowledge, and who can install better production methods can raise production without necessarily increasing group satisfaction. On the other hand, a supervisor who can motivate his employees and keep them satisfied with his leadership can gain high production in spite of technical difficulties and environmental obstacles.

CLIMATE AND SUPERVISION

Climate, the intangible environment of an organization made up of attitudes, beliefs, and traditions, plays a large part in morale, productivity, and supervision. Usually when we speak of climate and its relationship to morale and productivity, we talk about the merits of *democratic* versus *authoritarian* climate. Employees seem to produce more and have higher morale in a democratic climate, whereas in an authoritarian climate, the reverse seems to be true or so the researchers tell us. We would do well to determine what these terms mean to supervision.

Perhaps most of our difficulty in understanding and applying these concepts comes from our emotional reactions to the words themselves. For example, authoritarian climate is usually painted as the very blackest kind of dictatorship. This is not surprising, because we are usually expected to believe that it is invariably bad. Conversely, democratic climate is drawn to make the driven snow look impure by comparison.

Now these descriptions are most probably true when we talk about our political processes, or town meetings, or freedom of speech. However, the same labels have been used by social scientists in other contexts and have also been applied to government and business organizations, without it, it seems, any recognition that the meanings and their social values may have changed somewhat

For example, these labels were used in experiments conducted in an informal classroom setting using 11-year-old boys as subjects. The descriptive labels applied to the climate of the setting as well as the type of leadership practiced. When these labels were transferred to a management setting, it seems that many presumed that they principally meant the king of leadership rather than climate. We can see that there is a great difference between the experimental and management settings and that leadership practices for one might be inappropriate for the other.

It is doubtful that formal work organizations can be anything but authoritarian, in that goals are set by management and a hierarchy exists through which decisions and orders from the top are transmitted downward. Organizations are authoritarian by structure and need; direction and control are placed in the hands of a few in order to gain fast and efficient decision making. Now this does not mean to describe a dictatorship. It is merely the recognition of the fact that direction of organizational affairs comes from above. It should be noted that leadership in some natural groups is, in this sense, authoritarian.

Granting that formal organizations have this kind of authoritarian leadership, can there be a democratic climate? Certainly there can be, but we would want to define and delimit this term. A more realistic meaning of democratic climate in organizations is the use of permissive and participatory methods in management-employee relations. That is, a mutual exchange of information and explanation with the granting of individual freedom within certain restricted and defined limits. However, it is not our purpose to debate the merits of authoritarianism versus democracy. We recognize that within the small work group there is a need for freedom from constraint and an increase in participation in order to achieve organizational goals within the framework of the organizational movement.

Another aspect of climate is best expressed by this familiar, and true, saying: actions speak louder than words. Of particular concern to us is this effect of management climate on the behavior of supervisors, particularly in employee-centered activities.

There have been reports of disappointment with efforts to make supervisors ore employee-centered. Managers state that, since research has shown ways of improving human relations, supervisors should begin to practice these methods. Usually a training course in human relations is established; and supervisors are given this training. Managers then sit back and wait for the expected improvements, only to find that there are none.

If we wish to produce changes in the supervisor's behavior, the climate must be made appropriate and rewarding to the changed behavior. This means that top-level attitudes and behavior cannot deny or contradict the change we are attempting to effect. Basic changes in organizational behavior cannot be made with any permanence, unless we provide an environment that is receptive to the changes and rewards those persons who do change.

IMPROVING SUPERVISION

Anyone who has read this far might expect to find *A Dozen Rules for Dealing With Employees* or *29 Steps to Supervisory Success*. We will not provide such a list.

Simple rules suffer from their simplicity. They ignore the complexities of human behavior. Reliance upon rules may cause supervisors to concentrate on superficial aspects of their relations with employees. It may preclude genuine understanding.

The supervisor who relies on a list of rules tends to think of people in mechanistic terms. In a certain situation, he uses *Rule No. 3*. Employees are not treated as thinking and feeling persons, but rather as figures in a formula: Rule 3 applied to employee X = Production.

Employees usually recognize mechanical manipulation and become dissatisfied and resentful. They lose faith in, and respect for, their supervisor, and this may be reflected in lower morale and productivity.

We do not mean that supervisors must become social science experts if they wish to improve. Reports of current research indicate that there are two major parts of their job which can be strengthened through self-improvement: (1) Work planning, including technical skills, and (2) motivation of employees.

The most effective supervisors combine excellence in the administrative and technical aspects of their work with friendly and considerate personal relations with their employees.

## CRITICAL PERSONAL RELATIONS

Later in this chapter we shall talk about administrative aspects of supervision, but first let us comment on *friendly and considerate personal relations*. We have discussed this subject throughout the preceding chapters, but we want to review some of the critical supervisory influences on personal relations.

Closeness of Supervision: The closeness of supervision has an important effect on productivity and morale. Mann and Dent found that supervisors of low-producing units supervise very closely, while high-producing supervisors exercise only general supervision. It was found that the low-producing supervisors:

- check on employees more frequently
- give more detailed and frequent instructions
- limit employee's freedom to do job in own way

Workers who felt less closely supervised reported that they were better satisfied with their jobs and the company. We should note that the manner or attitude of the supervisor has an important bearing on whether employees perceive supervision as being close or general.

These findings are another way of saying that supervision does not mean standing over the employee and telling him what to do and when and how to do it. The more effective supervisor tells his employees what is required, giving general instructions.

## COMMUNICATION

Supervisors of high-production units consider communication as one of the most important aspects of their job. Effective communication is used by these supervisors to achieve better interpersonal relations and improved employee motivation. Low-production supervisors do not rate communications as highly important.

High-producing supervisors find that an important aid to more effective communication is listening. They are ready to listen to both personal problems or interests and questions about the work. This does not mean that they are *nosey* or meddle in their employees' personal lives, but rather that they show a willingness to listen, and do listen, if their employees wish to discuss problems.

These supervisors inform employees about forthcoming changes in work; they discuss agency policy with employees; and they make sure that each employee knows how well he is doing. What these supervisors do is use two-way communication effectively. Unless the supervisor freely imparts information, he will not receive information in return.

Attitudes and perception are frequently affected by communication or the lack of it. Research surveys reveal that many supervisors are not aware of their employees' attitudes, nor do they know what personal reactions their supervision arouses. Through frank discussion with employees, they have been surprised to discover employee beliefs about which they were ignorant. Discussion sometimes reveals that the supervisor and his employees have totally different impressions about the same event. The supervisor should be constantly on the alert for misconceptions about his words and deeds. He must remember that, although his actions are perfectly clear to himself, they may be, and frequently are, viewed differently by employees.

Failure to communicate information results in misconceptions and false assumptions. What you say and how you say it will strongly affect your employees' attitudes and perceptions. By giving them available information, you can prevent misconceptions; by discussion, you may be able to change attitudes; by questioning, you can discover what the perceptions and assumptions really are. And it need hardly be added that actions should conform very closely to words.

If we were to attempt to reduce the above discussion on communication to rules, we would have a long list which would be based on one cardinal principle: Don't make assumptions!

- Don't assume that your employees know; tell them.
- Don't assume that you know how they feel; find out.
- Don't assume that they understand; clarify.

## 20 SUPERVISORY HINTS

1. Avoid inconsistency.
2. Always give employees a chance to explain their action before taking disciplinary action. Don't allow too much time for a "cooling off" period before disciplining an employee.
3. Be specific in your criticisms.
4. Delegate responsibility wisely.
5. Do not argue or lose your temper, and avoid being impatient.
6. Promote mutual respect and be fair, impartial, and open-minded.
7. Keep in mind that asking for employees' advice and input can be helpful in decision making.
8. If you make promises, keep them.
9. Always keep the feelings, abilities, dignity and motives of your staff in mind.
10. Remain loyal to your employees' interests.
11. Never criticize employees in front of others, or treat employees like children.
12. Admit mistakes. Don't place blame on your employees, or make excuses.
13. Be reasonable in your expectations, give complete instructions, and establish well-planned goals.
14. Be knowledgeable about office details and procedures, but avoid becoming bogged down in details.
15. Avoid supervising too closely or too loosely. Employees should also view you as an approachable supervisor.
16. Remember that employees' personal problems may affect job performance, but become involved only when appropriate.
17. Work to develop workers, and to instill a feeling of cooperation while working toward mutual goals.
18. Do not overpraise or underpraise, be properly appreciative.
19. Never ask an employee to discipline someone for you.
20. A complaint, even if unjustified, should be taken seriously.

## NOTES